Challenges for Saudi Women in Unconventional Jobs

Hakem Amin Sabbag

Table of Contents

List of Tables

List of Figures

Abbreviations

FLFP	Female labor force participation
KSA	Kingdom of Saudi Arabia
GCC	Gulf Cooperation Council
HRM	Human resources management
SCCT	Social Cognitive Career Theory
STEM	Science, Technology, Engineering, and Mathematics
TYS	Third year STEM students
FM	Faculty members
FYS	Foundation year STEM track students
ERIC	Ethical Research Involving Children

Abstract

Advancing awareness of the workforce and job issues faced by women in the KSA will encourage HRM departments to enhance Saudi women's work experience by implementing more gender-friendly work environments, practices, and processes. Therefore, the researcher decided to implement this research to shed light on the role of Saudi women working in community development, to identify the most important challenges and issues facing Saudi women working in new unconventional jobs, and to discuss methods that can be followed to reduce these challenges and issues. To achieve this, the researcher used a descriptive-analytical approach and qualitative research methods (interviews). The interviews were conducted with 10 Saudi women working in new, non-traditional jobs. The study reached a number of results, most notably that Saudi society still rejects the work of Saudi women and their participation in the labor market. The results also confirmed that the Kingdom of Saudi Arabia seeks to provide suitable job opportunities for Saudi women and to integrate them into the labor market. In addition, the results confirmed that the family plays an important role in supporting working Saudi women and helping them achieve career and professional excellence. In light of this, the researcher recommended the necessity of changing Saudi society's view of working Saudi women. The need to make many transformative changes in employment methods and to achieve equal employment opportunities between women and men.

Keywords: Saudi women, challenges, unconventional, job, support, new.

Chapter 1: Introduction

Introduction

During the past two decades, Women's proportion in management and leadership positions has grown (Broadbridge, 2010; Davidson and Burke, 2011; Powell, 2010). Nevertheless, due to barriers such as poor of mentors and networks (Bagilhole and White, 2011; Kanter, 1977), work-life conflict (Broadbridge, 2009; Lewis, 2002), institutional systemic problems (Kanter, 1977), and perceptions of gender roles, there is substantial evidence that women's career advancement to leadership positions appears difficult (Davidson and Burke, 2011; Fagenson, 1990).

As a result of increased women's enrollment at all educational levels and in different fields of employment and facets of public life in Saudi Arabia, women's involvement in senior management roles and in the decision-making process in the public and private sectors has increased over the last 10 years. Recent advances have shown that Saudi Arabia's policymakers and development plans have a strong strategic path towards an even greater role for women in public life and leading roles in the public domain. Evidence indicates that, despite the significant role of women in Saudi society, women in leadership roles face a different fact from their male colleagues due to institutional, personal, and cultural obstacles that hinder their efficiency as leaders (Al-Ahmadi, 2011).

In Saudi Arabia, women represent nearly half of the total population or human resources (Alkhateeb & Sultan, 2014). Today, more than 90% of Saudi women who engage actively in the workplace hold secondary or university qualifications, in 2006, 57% of university graduates were women in Saudi Arabia, and this growing level of education is the main factor in increasing female employment. This isn't to say that merely having a degree helps Saudi women to enter the job market unfortunately, it does not. Nonetheless, according to Abdul Wahid Al-Humaid, Deputy Minister of Labor, several homeless women are highly qualified: 78.3% are university graduates. In comparison, 76% of unemployed men only have secondary or lower learning (AlMunajjed, 2010).

In recent times, The Saudi government has also recognized the importance of Saudi women. The government paid particular attention to raising the position of women in various areas of growth, especially economic growth. The acceptance by the Saudi Government of the United Nations Charter to help women politically, to provide a sound atmosphere for women to work, to open a women 's office in the labor branches under the Ministry of Labor, to improve women's ability and to increase their participation in economic actions. High targeted growth rates call for complete and effective utilization of all economic resources, including human capital. Because women make up about half of the human capital, their active involvement in economic activities is of vital importance as this will not only enhance their knowledge and competitiveness but also minimize the country's reliance on foreign labor (Alkhateeb & Sultan, 2014).

Consequently, undertaking cross-country studies to discover the complexities of job issues and obstacles to career advancement for women would be important in the future. Future research may also have the design of mixed, systemic research to address the challenges of involving Saudi women in social and labor law research (Al-Asfour, 2012).

Due to cultural socialization and cultural beliefs, Saudi women do not have many opportunities compared to other women; they only began working in several sectors that were occupied by men for a long time last few years when King Abdullah Bin Abdelaziz declared in 2011 that Saudi women are allowed to work for shops selling women's necessities. When the structure fails to drive these women forward, nevertheless, society drives women down and does not help them (Hakem, 2017).

Background

Few researches in the Kingdom of Saudi Arabia have investigated the work issues and career obstacles faced by women. Hakem (2017) analyzed Saudi women's position in relation to the labor market, take into consideration social inequalities, religious perspective, government role, and cultural complexities.

Al-Asfour et al. (2017) were conducted in-depth research on the perspectives of working Saudi women. The researchers used qualitative methods based on 12 semi-structured, in-depth interviews with Saudi women. The results identified a large number of influential systemic and attitudinal social and organizational obstacles to Saudi women progressing in paid jobs. Such obstacles include, among others, lack of mobility; the salience of gender stereotypes; workplace gender discrimination; restricted opportunity for expansion, development and career advancement; disproportionate workload induced by lack of family work balance; and gender-based difficulties related to pregnancy management.

Al-bakr et al. (2017) explored Saudi university students' perspectives on shifting gender roles as they are influenced by women's rights, education, jobs, and public-sphere participation. Outcomes from a questionnaire distributed between 4,455 males and females suggest that students are positive and enthusiastic about gender equality change, but there is still opposition from those with traditional ideas.

Al-Rasheed (2013) points out that there are shifts in the condition. Due to the arbitration between society and religion, approved by King Abdullah, Saudi women are increasingly active in the public sphere (Fatany, 2013). By growing access to jobs and nominating women to the

Shoura Council in January 2013, he endorsed women's liberation (Jordan, 2013). Later in 2015, for the first time in local elections, women voted independently, suggesting that the opinions of both women and men were significant for the growth of Saudi Arabian society.

According to Alahmadi (2011) In spite of the considerable role of women in Saudi society, evidence suggests that women in leadership positions are facing a different reality from their male counterparts due to organizational, personal, and cultural challenges that impede their effectiveness as leaders. This study aimed to describe the obstacles women leaders faced in Saudi Arabia's governmental departments via a questionnaire of 160 women leaders. The results indicated that the major issues are: systemic problems, lack of capital, and lack of confidence, while personal and cultural problems ranked third, contrary to popular understanding.

In Saudi Arabia, which has a distinctive gender-segregated culture, one augmented by cultural, religious, and social norms, Sani (2018) examined the inclusion of women in STEM education and professions. This research also explores the factors on the decisions of girls to pursue STEM education and professions by using a mixed-method approach that reflects on participants' lived experiences. Questionnaires were provided at one public university to 352 women participants. Of these, 312 were STEM track students (FYS) in the founding year, 30 were third-year STEM students (TYS), and 10 were members of the university faculty (FM). Analysis of the survey data showed that the ambitions of students for STEM professions start as early as grade 4; mathematics is the favorite academic subject, and medicine is the most desired occupation. Semi-structured interviews with a total of 35 participants were carried out: FYS (20), TYS (10), and FM (5). A review of the qualitative data found that in public schools, girls do not face subject-related gender stereotypes. Nonetheless, though they are empowered to learn all science subjects, only the most educated in high school and university can pursue the science route. It was also clear that career education in Saudi Arabian schools is insufficient and students seldom receive career guidance in school, while their parents and extended family receive unprecedented guidance and advice. Giddens' Structuration Theory gained evidential support from the results of this analysis. It shows that social and cultural changes in women-only and family spheres are commonplace, where girls' agentic acts are allowed and ultimately contributing to their empowerment within them.

Almujahid (2009) described the Saudi government's main achievements in the field of female public education. It also discusses the problems that obstruct the advancement of female education and the active participation of women in the labor market. Finally, it proposes a range of policy changes and suggestions that, if adopted, will lead to the establishment of high-quality women's education, a more advanced and knowledge-based society, Saudi women's involvement in society, and the reorganizing of women's socio-cultural experience in Saudi society.

Problem

In an economic growth, female labor force participation (FLFP) plays an important role. As a growing economy, the Kingdom of Saudi Arabia (KSA) relies primarily on men instead of women to reach its growth goals. Saudi FLFPs are exceedingly small over a span of 50 years (Naseem & Dhruva, 2017). Men and women face dramatically different incomes and rates of participation and jobs in the labor force and prefer to focus on various sectors and occupations. FLFP remains extremely poor in Saudi Arabia, despite the latest improvements. In addition, participation rises have worsened female unemployment as job availability has struggled to keep pace with higher FLFP. Saudi women who do find jobs remain focused in a few sectors (Naseem & Dhruva, 2017).

Despite the global attention drawn by women's professions, awareness about women's employment is limited in the Arab world. The academic research and studies of several academics seek to recognize the careers of women in the US and European countries, paying no attention to women in the Arab region's developing countries. Also in the face of rising interest in Arab women, most studies concentrate on particular countries like Lebanon (Tlaiss and Dirani, 2015; Tlaiss, 2014b) and the United Arab Emirates (Tlaiss, 2013, 2014a), With limited work in the Kingdom of Saudi Arabia (KSA) explicitly on women. Given the Gulf Cooperation Council (GCC) countries' commonalities, each nation has its own structural realities and distinctive features that require separate studies to gain insight into country-specific settings (Sidani and Gardner, 2000), Particularly women 's experiences in each country. This research gap reduces awareness not only of the Arab women's experiences but also of the interplay among women's employment and social systems and business frameworks.

The lack of expertise often adversely affects the country's enhanced of human resources management (HRM) (Tlaiss and Dirani, 2015), which is already lagging in compared with other areas. Advancing awareness of the workforce and job issues faced by women in the KSA will encourage HRM departments to enhance Saudi women's work experience by implementing more gender-friendly work environments, practices, and processes. Therefore, the researcher decided to implement this research to shed light on the role of Saudi women working in community development, to identify the most important challenges and issues facing Saudi women working in new unconventional jobs, and to discuss methods that can be followed to reduce these challenges and issues.

Questions

The current research problem can be represented by the following main question:

- What are the challenges and issues that Saudi women face when they are assigned to high, new, and challenging positions?

There are several sub-questions that will be discussed in the current research, the most important of which are the following:

- What are the procedures that can be followed to overcome the challenges facing working Saudi women?
- What is the role of working Saudi women in the development of society culturally and economically?
- What are the factors that affect the acceptance of Saudi women working in new unconventional jobs?
- What is the role of the family in supporting and supporting Saudi women working in new unconventional jobs?

Aim and Objectives

The current research seeks to discuss the challenges and issues faced by Saudi women when they are appointed to new unconventional jobs such as aviation, engineering, art, and architecture, besides that, the research seeks to achieve the following goals:

- Highlighting the procedures that can be taken to overcome the challenges facing working with Saudi women.
- Disclosure of the role of Saudi women working in the development of society culturally and economically.
- Discuss the factors that affect the acceptance of Saudi women in new unconventional jobs.

- Disclosure of the role of the family in supporting and supporting Saudi women working in sensitive locations.

Operational Definitions

This study included a number of key terms that serve the purpose of the study, below we review definitions of these terms:

Saudi Arabia: Saudi Arabia: is the largest GCC country by geographical area, population, and size of the economy. The KSA shares border with Jordan, Iraq, Kuwait, Qatar, Oman, Yemen, and the United Arab Emirates, and is connected by a waterway to the Kingdom of Bahrain. In 2020, the population of KSA was estimated at 48 million (Al-Asfour et al., 2017).

Unconventional jobs: it is new, unconventional jobs in many modern scientific and technological fields such as medicine, medicine, engineering, science, and other modern industries.

Limitations

There were a number of limitations affecting this study, including:

I. There is a lack of willingness to participate in the interviews, due to the timing of data collection.

II. This study was limited to the experiences of Saudi women leaders in new, Unconventional jobs.

III. The interviews were conducted electronically through the Internet due to the Coronavirus pandemic afflicting the world. This imposes restrictions on internet connection and connection quality.

IV. The inability to survey and notice the participants' reactions and gestures during the interview due to online interviews.

V.   There may be a limit to understanding the significance of the issue. Saudi women may not want to participate in the study because they do not yet realize the importance of their observations. To address this limitation, the researcher must clearly explain the purpose of the study and emphasize the importance of collecting such data for the future growth of their community.

VI.   There was a limited number of posts. The number of respondents has an estimated 10 Saudi women.

Outline

The current study will be prepared based on a set of sequential and ordered steps that can be identified in the following points:

- Review previous studies and literature related to the current research topic.
- Providing an integrated theoretical framework covering all research variables.
- Defining the research problem and its purpose.
- Selecting a population and sample search.
- Choosing the research tools and statistical methods that will be used in the research.
- Research tools design.
- Distribution of the research tools to the research sample.
- Primary data collection from research tools.
- Statistical processing of primary information.
- Analysis of the results.
- Provide a set of findings and recommendations.
- Presenting some future proposals that focus on developing the research topic.

Organization of Study

This study is divided into five chapters. Chapter one includes the introduction, research problem, research questions, the aim and objectives, and significance of the study, timeline, and definitions of terms used.

Chapter two includes a review of the literature related to (a) Islamic Schooling in the Cultural West (b) The Challenges Faced by Muslim children in British Cultural. (c) the Issues Concerning School Choice for Muslim children.

In chapter three, the methodology used to include research design, procedures, sample selection, data collection, and data analysis is described.

Chapter three describes the methodology employed involving research design, procedures, sample selection, data processing, and data analysis. The results of data analysis are reported in chapter four, the data analyzing findings are reported.

Chapter 2: Literature Review

Introduction

This part review discusses and critically examines the relevant literature and empirical

research that encompasses the theme of the research and its variables. According to the purpose

of this study, which aimed at investigating the challenges and issues that Saudi women face

when they are assigned to high, new, and challenging positions.

This part is a theoretical framework that is concerned with issues related to the challenges

and issues faced by Saudi women when they are appointed to new unconventional jobs such as

Women and work in Saudi Arabia, Saudi Women between the Past and the Present, Islamic

Point of View, The present generation with the vision of the Kingdom 2030 and new positions,

Saudi women's empowerment, Social and Cultural Difficulties, and Saudi women's work

challenges, barriers to career advancement, and so on.

Women and work in Saudi Arabia

Women make up almost 50 % of the population in Saudi Arabia, but their contribution to

estimated economic activity is well below their potential. In particular, the role of women is

considered to be central to preserving the structure of the family and thus of society (Saqib,

2016).

Saudi women constitute half, if not more, of Saudi society. She is the man's partner in

social life. As she is his mother, sister, daughter, wife, and social and financial partner, she is

interested in the development, growth, and promotion of change and prosperity in the

community. (Ibrahim, 2013). Furthermore, women are closely linked to the state-oriented

economic and human resource growth policies that Saudi society has experienced when engaging

in the labor market (Al-Yousef, 2005).

Saudi women also remain excluded from full social participation In fact, Saudi Arabia remains one of the countries that suffer from gender discrimination. The nation has a very high Global Gender Gap ranking, ranked 141st in 2018 out of 149 nations, and the third-lowest of 18 countries in the region of the Middle East and North Africa. In addition, the nation has regressed in narrowing its gender gap in contrast with recent years. While the number of working women in the private industry raised by 130% between 2012 and 2016, its education and political empowerment indexes (93 and 127 out of 149) continue to be behind the economic engagement and incentive index score (145 out of 149) (Gulf News, 2017; World Economic Forum, 2018).

The Ministry of Labour and Social Development launched many projects under the National Transformation Program 2020 that would create 141,000 new jobs that would enable women to work from home (Gulf News, 2017, emphasis added). The latter knowledge indicates that these changes would only adhere to current hierarchical constraints without removing the key causes of exclusion. In the future years, economic engagement and the opportunity index could be increased, though women will remain under-represented in several sectors of the economy (Topal, 2019).

Saudi Women between the Past and the Present

However, from a conventional Saudi cultural viewpoint, for women high school graduates, "housewife" was the acceptable and expected role, and "the home" was the right place for women. In general, the societal attitudes in Saudi Arabia did not enable women to work with men or in public. Historically, education was exclusively for boys; the Saudi government only formally discussed the question of girls' education after 1959, and most families were not involved in girls' education at that time (Al-Rawaf & Simmons, 1991).

A small part of the Saudi labor market is made up of Saudi women, and in its early phases, Saudiisation did not identify women intensively. Several of the industries addressed have not employed women at all. 26.3% of female university graduates were unemployed in 2006, and 34.8% were unemployed in 2013 (Central Department of Statistics and Information, 2013).

In hindering women's jobs, Saudi culture and norms play an important role. Moreover, women's occupations are limited areas, with many employees in education and few in medicine. Recently, as trained women have come to be seen as a previously lost resource, the Saudi government began to concentrate more on women's jobs. Saudisation will prove its efficacy in reducing women's unemployment if it is successfully introduced and provides hundreds of job opportunities for women. Women will have the ability to engage in the labor market and have their own spaces, rights, and resources for their voices to be heard through the successful implementation of Saudisation (Alghamdi, 2014).

In the past decade, patterns have shifted towards Saudi female freedom in order to engage alongside men in competitive and professional life. Women also excelled in the healthcare, government, literature, and media industries (Al-Rasheed, 2018). In the area of literature, a great change has been noted. In using the pen as their weapon of choice and describing feminism, Saudi women have empowered themselves to a great extent. In addition, they clarified the significance of this phase of feminism in connection to their rights, education, and a substantially social networking shift in Saudi Arabia (Ammar, 2018; Alqahtani, 2020).

According to Dunham (2013), many Saudi women enjoy luxuries other women do not. Numerous Saudi women, for instance, enjoy the privilege of studying abroad and getting access to public scholarships that pay for their education. Several Saudi women enjoy the privilege of becoming residents of a nation rich in oil resources. Many Saudi women are also conscious of their cultural heritage and are especially proud that the custodian of the two holy mosques is the King of Saudi Arabia. These items have served to fund several Saudi women's educational and work-related opportunities. Conversely, that is not to suggest that all Saudi women are benefiting from this oil wealth or their rich cultural heritage. Nevertheless, they do not consider themselves to be the most marginalized and downtrodden of all Arab and Muslim people.

Islamic Point of View

According to Islam, Males and females are equivalent in their marital status. As before marriage, both maintain their respective surnames as they were. After marriage, a female does not follow the surname of her husband, as if she were bound to him. In relation to what they receive from their own efforts or any other valid means, Islam grants equal rights of ownership to both males and females: men will benefit from what they earn and females will benefit from what they earn (Al-Khayat, 2003).

The Prophet of Islam (Peace be upon him) gave women a peaceful role with a divine path that could not be imagined in the pre-Islamic era. Consequently, women were entitled in a genuinely Islamic society to enjoy full freedom of will as persons and to earn their social, economic, and political rights like men. The Holy Quran regards both males and females as persons in the same way (Elius, 2010).

Islam offers women a place of honor and dignity, with explicitly defined rights and responsibilities, from the Muslim viewpoint. In the aspects of marriage, divorce, and inheritance, the Qur'än offers legal guarantees that are considered to represent a significant enhancement over the women's condition in pre-Islamic society (Smith, 1979).

Muslim women gained freedom of movement in the early days of Islamic history and engaged in many fields of social life. In both civil and military life, they cooperated with men.

Independence made it possible for women to grow their latent powers. They have been able to make full use of their ability through social structures and the environment. "That's why women have excelled in war, literature, oratory, public administration, music, theology (Kalam), jurisprudence (Fiqh), Hadith Studies (I'lmul Hadith), mysticism (Tasawwuf), poetry, and so on" (Elius, 2010).

Since early Muslim society gave women their basic rights to education and self-development, several women have been able to leave their mark on historical pages. Out of the hundreds of such illustrious females, some are listed here. Ayesha (R), the wife of the prophet Muhammad (PBUH), for instance, was a woman of profound erudition. In order to learn Islamic law, theology, and hadith, several Sahaba (companions of the Prophet) and Tabeeyeen (direct followers of the Sahaba) came to her. Zainab (R), Hazrat Ali's (K) daughter, was a great Islamic scholar of theology. The two Islamic scholars, Fatima Binte Abbas and Sikha Sayeeda used to come to the mosque daily to give Islamic theology lectures. History documents the names of several female warriors who fought on the battlefields against enemies. In several fights, even Hazrat Aisha (R) took an active part. Umme Atyqah was a courageous lady who in seven battles followed the Prophet (PBUH). In the battle of Yarmuk, Wairyh, Muawia's niece, led a contingent of women. In the field of spirituality, Muslim females have left their mark. In the early Islamic period, some prominent Sufi saints also emerged among women (Alam 1984: 305-11).

Islam and Saudi Arabia are closely intertwined, and the close-knit connection has been reflected on by several theorists. For instance, Denman and Hilal (2011: p. 304) explained that "the Islamic religion is regarded as part of the Saudi identification as much as the long-standing history of the country as part of the greater Arab Peninsula". Furthermore, Ochsenwald (1981: p.

274) wrote: "In Saudi Arabia, Islam has been the omnipresent and dominant force in public life since its inception".

One of the most traditional Muslim societies in the world is known to be Saudi Arabia. Indeed, Saudi Arabia is the only theocratic Arab country where Islam is closely linked to the government. This framework is primarily embodied by governmental and male roles who see the foundation for their identity as biology (being born a woman) and social hierarchy (women's status and roles in Saudi Arabia).

Because of the Wahabi interpretation of shari'a laws that govern all facets of life in Saudi Arabia and which have remained largely unchanged, the essentialist paradigm is placed on women in Saudi Arabia and by the assigned roles and assumptions established by a culture that emphasizes the role of Saudi women as wives and mothers (Miller-Rosser, Chapman, & Francis, 2006).

Yamani (2000: p. 96) found out that "while interpretations of 'right' Islamic conduct affect all parts of society, local customs, norms, and tribal traditions actually dictate the functions of women and are enforced by the family framework". According to Doumato (2010: p. 425), "gender inequality is integrated into the governmental and social systems of Saudi Arabia and is central to the state-supported understanding of Islam in the region, which derives from a literal reading of the Koran and Sunna".

The Saudi Kingdom declared towards the end of 2017 that a phase of changing its Islamic practices would be pursued. These changes are said to turn "ultra-conservative Islam" into "moderate Islam." It was also reported that this version of Islam would cause a shift in the role of women in the country. The Crown Prince Mohammad bin Salman ordered changes in September 2017 that enable women to enter cinemas and sports stadiums and drive without a male guardian present in the car with a license ('Saudi Arabia to allow', 2017). So many Saudi experts met in Riyadh in November 2017 for an event called "Empowering women is motivating society" to examine the future changes ("National experts meet", 2017). Understandably, the Western media and foreign organizations welcomed these efforts to congratulate the Kingdom on its drive towards women's empowerment (Topal, 2019).

The present generation with the Kingdom vision 2030 and new positions

Despite high living standards and educational achievement between women, Saudi Arabia has the biggest gender job disparity in the world. The Saudi government solves this issue in the recently launched National Development Plan Vision 2030, which seeks to rebuild the economy to reduce the kingdom's oil dependence (Swaantje, 2018).

King Salman bin Abdulaziz, along with Crown Prince Mohammad bin Salman, recently unveiled and suggested a vision for 2030. Vision 2030 focuses on introducing a knowledge-based Saudi economy that will allow Saudi Arabia's young people to fulfill their dreams of reaching their goals through education and jobs (Mitchell & Alfuraih, 2018). In addition, lifting the ban on women's driving has also played a crucial role in promoting Saudi women's freedom in the nation. In Saudi Arabia, there are a handful of women who have benefited from this legislation because they were traditionally dependent on their drivers and public transport. It should be noted that this important change is also part of the vision of King Salman for 2030 to advance women's empowerment (Krane & Majid, 2018).

The Vision 2030 is an optimistic multi-dimensional improving agenda that is focused on three key elements: "A vibrant community, a productive economy, an ambitious country" (Vision 2030, 2016). Its implementation includes all government bodies, dividing obligations according to their various spheres of operation. For example, the Ministry of Labour and Social

Development is mainly accountable for the implementation of labor market policies under Vision 2030. One of the key aspects of the comprehensive Vision 2030 is the incorporation of Saudi women into the workforce. The Saudi government aims to expand the Saudi economy and open up alternative economic sectors in order to reduce its reliance on the oil industry. In this regard, women present a huge untapped potential.

Studies indicate that the possible rise in the participation of women similarly in the workforce as men may be as high as 47% of the GDP of the MENA region (McKinsey, 2015). Consequently, there are obviously good economic benefits for Saudi Arabia to have women in the workforce. The Saudization and Nitaqat policies put in place to increase the share of Saudi nationals in the private industry, who are currently predominantly employed by expatriates, are instances of such policies. Studies indicate that such quota-based strategies have been relatively successful but that FLFP has not achieved a sustained increase because they have not tackled social systemic factors that create obstacles to women's job opportunities in the labor market (Abeer, 2016).

In order to reduce the kingdom's dependency on the oil industry, the recently released National Development Plan Vision 2030 seeks to restructure the Saudi economy. The Vision focuses heavily on growing FLFP, re-sparking the discussion on the subject in academia and the international media as well. Nevertheless, although a lot of research has been carried out exploring the various constraints of FLFP in Saudi Arabia, due to the novelty of the growth agenda, there is a lack of research on how the problem is being tackled under Vision 2030.

According to Alsharif (2019) despite the encouraging trends of the last few decades, women in the private industry are still under-represented in the workforce. The purpose of Vision 2030 is to make it possible to increase FLFP from 10% to 30% by 2030, based on the fact that Saudi women are now very well educated and that women from the lower strata of society who have access to higher education have acquired a collection of skills that can provide access to various maritime sectors thanks to the help they have earned.

Studies have been carried out to show the after-effects of permission to drive for Saudi women, which showed a general state of happiness between women in order to fulfill their dreams of independence. As for freedom, women were also found to be more enthusiastic than men (Al-Ghalib et al, 2018). In addition, Vision 2030 plays a role in enhancing women's opportunities in different sectors, like nursing. Historically, in order to satisfy the requirements of home and hospital care, foreigners have been working on a wide scale. The emergence of the 2030 vision, nevertheless, has given Saudi women the opportunity to pursue an education in this field and play a major role in developing the country's economy (Al-Dossary, 2018).

Saudi Women's Empowerment

Empowerment can be reached through access to expertise, adequate authority and access to information, as well as self-development, recognition and support, involvement in the setting of priorities and policy decisions, and the identification of methods and techniques (Kubaisi, 2004). In all of these dimensions, all failure would therefore result in a lack of empowerment and, therefore, inadequate leadership. According to Effendi (2003), Empowerment increases the moral and physical sense of belonging and association with the organization, leaving a positive impact on the individual's psyche and increases emotions of respect and relevance to the institution.

Today, Saudi women's empowerment in the labor market has become an urgent necessity for their leadership position to be fulfilled at this time, more than ever, owing to the segregated work system in which women, apart from men, are completely separated. There are no men in these parts to do the lead there actually. In the present situation, man leaders relay instructions to female leaders whose highest position in the women's section is a vice-dean or a vice-chair, and many female leaders are not comfortable talking to a man who is not a member of the family (Al Ghamdi, 2016). These truths stem from the cultural norms and values that lead women in academia to refuse to take those roles. Women leaders, irrespective of their authority or role, avoid interaction with male leaders, requiring them to rely on paper and, less frequently, electronic communications, which are undesirable behaviors that place all leaders in a strictly bureaucratic situation. In the face of the vulnerability of electronic communication in several developing universities, this is particularly problematic (Al Ghamdi, 2016).

Theories

For Saudi women, their career-related self-efficacy is primarily influenced by the educational process and cultural values. It prevents them from being extremely advanced in certain fields or from succeeding in or choosing unconventional careers. Despite the many contributions made by previous studies that were included in this research, the majority of them did not include the scientific theories that support the work of women. Although there are many of these theories, this research will be implemented based because of several scientific theories, the most important of which are:

1. Social cognitive career theory.

Literally, the Social Cognitive Theory of Bandura (1986) is the cornerstone of the Social Cognitive Career Theory (SCCT). In determining results, the fundamental belief and definition of the theory are focused on the interconnection among personal, cognitive, and environmental parameters. The function of cognitive parameters is emphasized by social cognitive theory; Lent et al. (1994) claim that the three social assessments of factors of confidence in self-efficacy, the expectation of performance, and target choice have an outstanding impact on the SCCT.

Lent, Brown, and Hackett (1994) have formulated this theory, which focused on three main aspects: (a) how to grow basic education and career interests, (b) how to make educational and career decisions, and (c) how to reach educational and career achievements. For career growth, the researchers include 3 elements: (a) motivation, (b) career choice method includes selecting a target, and (c) career achievement success and persistence (Lent et al., 1994). These three measures are affected by the self-efficacy and perceptions of the result of an individual.

This career model emphasizes the role of self-efficacy in career growth as a predictor. Self-effectiveness is established through the experience of life (gender, race, disability, personality, and predisposition). Moreover, External influences may have a significant impact on the career choice of a person. Lent et al. (1994) also indicated that contextual affordances include (perceived obstacles or assistance) help explain why an individual might not be involved in a big job (Lent et al., 1994; Swanson & Fouad, 2010).

2. Super's developmental theory.

Super presented one of the most prominent work theories of the 20th century in 1953 (as quoted in Swanson & Fouad, 2010). This hypothesis was based on the significance of the individual's self-concept, which evolves through experience over time. According to Super, self-conception is created from influences like mental and physical growth, personal experience, and social learning experiences. Super suggested five stages of life that individuals commonly go through, and establish features during each phase.

The phases are growth period (age 4–13): self-concept creation and behavior creation. Exploration (age 14–24): acquiring professional decision-making skills and experience.

Establishment (age 25–44): create a career and work-life balance which includes stabilizing, consolidating, and progressing the career route. Maintenance (ages 45–65): continuous career progression. Disengagement (over 65 years of age): to rising productivity.

The theory also utilized the career maturity definition as a measure of a person's ability to perform the career development tasks expected at each level. Super's theory applied to foreign technical practitioners and scholars, as it takes notions like developmental phases, career maturity and role in life into account. Recent theoretical findings concentrate on the impact of social-cultural norms on personal choices. Cultural values and expectations are important for self-conception and job preferences (Leung, 2008; Swanson & Fouad, 2010).

Super's theory is a synthesis of the theory of level development and social role (Super et. al, 1996), which implies that throughout the career development phase, people move through five phases, like development, discovery, establishment, maintenance, and disengagement. It should be recognized that the theory of Super is not a static theory of stage in which the age of a person determines his or her progression from stage to stage, a mechanism known as max cycling.

Super proposed that movement through the five phases may be a fluid mechanism in which individuals across different periods of life recycle through those stages. This process is referred to as mini cycling by Super. For the purposes of this essay, within the context of its conventional occurrence through adolescence, the development level will be explored in detail (Kosine, & Lewis, 2008).

Social and Cultural Difficulties

In particular, women are responsible for multi-faceted roles that revolve around the home and family. They are constantly busy because of this and have a shortage of spare time, especially when they work both outside and inside the house. Their duties are likely to include caring for their spouse, children, and household but may also include other duties like promoting the career of their husbands or caring for their elders or sick family member (Gouthro, 2007). They also put their own interests at a lower priority by spending their time in meeting the needs of their families and children (Heenan, 2002).

Despite Saudi society's increased attention to female issues and to their educational level, the reality of their participation in the labor market remains poor, as some Saudi women are still suffering from poverty and widespread unemployment. In 2007, the unemployment level between women specifically in Saudi Arabia was around (26.6%), then it rose to reach (26.9%) in 2008 and continued to grow to reach (28.4%) in 2009, which is four times the rate of youth unemployment in 2009 (6.9%) (AL-Hazmi, Hammad, & AL-Shahrani, 2017).

Sometimes this is because most perceptions and social interaction strategies concentrate on the single role of the woman within the family and do not consider the multiplicity of her family's and community positions, which is negatively reflected on women, whether it causes her to leave for work mentally or culturally (Howaishah, 2010). The key reasons for the shrinking of the position of women in the labor markets are ideologies that oppose the work of women, the high birth rate, low job prospects, and illiteracy. Other causes of unemployment between females are the resistance of a large proportion of men to female's jobs, as well as their reluctance to do homework for disparaging purposes (Al-Ashqar 2013).

Few researches in the Kingdom of Saudi Arabia have investigated the work issues and career obstacles faced by women. Hakem (2017) analyzed Saudi women's position in relation to the labor market, take into consideration social inequalities, religious perspective, government role, and cultural complexities.

There are several barriers and restrictions facing women seeking unconventional careers that can hinder or obstruct their career growth. The lack of relevant learning opportunities and role models, poor beliefs in self-efficacy, ambiguous perceptions of performance, and cultural and social obstacles must always be addressed by those who want to engage in trade and development occupations. A theoretical basis for the evaluation of the career growth of these women is provided by Social Cognitive Career Theory (SCCT; Lent, Brown, & Hackett, 1994).

Saudi women's work challenges and barriers to career advancement

According to Al-Asfour et al. (2017), the responses of the Saudi women interviewed in this study illustrate a range of obstacles and difficulties that impede their career development. These results clearly demonstrate that a dynamic system of stressors affects Saudi women both at home and at work, like restricted opportunities for job and career development, disproportionate workload induced by a lack of family-work balance, pregnancy and mobility issues, lack of equality, and workplace gender inequality.

Previous studies have linked the lack of flexibility offered by their employers to the high rates of women leaving the workforce. The current study suggests that Saudi women who work for institutions that are responsive to their job challenges and build career pathways for them will enjoy higher employee loyalty, regardless of whether attitudes towards working women have changed or remain conventional.

Smith (2006) argues that it is important to provide a nationally recognized, job-training intervention that tackles multiple challenges in the workplace to empower women. Cultural barriers can be eliminated by recognizing the capacity of women at work; attitudinal barriers can be reduced by enhancing the trust, self-esteem, and comparative role of women; the barrier to qualifications can be overcome by providing higher education pathways and encouragement to continue learning, and institutional barriers can be overcome by providing alternative employee attendance policies (Smith, 2006).

Moreover, research studies indicated that Saudi Arabia's women's industries face many organizational deficiencies, including the lack of consistency in the organizational relationship among women's and men's divisions, inadequate communication, and subordination of women's sectors to the organizational chart (and in some cases not including women sectors in the organizational chart altogether), in addition to the subordination of women sections to the organizational structure (Almenkash et al., 2007).

Almenkash et al. (2007) suggest that insufficient coordination and inadequate information systems contribute to the widening divide among women's sectors and top leaders, in addition to the exclusion of women's sectors from the corporate headquarters activities, and the absence of involvement in strategic planning and academic decision-making and academic and administrative membership.

Another problem facing women leaders may be a lack of empowerment, which is expressed in their failure to control the decision-making process and achieve organizational goals due to the lack of empowerment instruments or techniques (Metcalfe, 2008). Evidence indicates a variety of variables that relate to the absence of female leaders' empowerment. These include lack of administrative performance, restricted opportunities for training, lack of opportunities for professional exchange, and collaboration with other organizations in order to obtain diverse experience, exclusion of women from certain policies and regulations, and involvement in decision-making (Almenkash et al. 2007), and lack of access to data (Sultan, 1994). Evidence also indicates that the quantity and standard of leadership training available to women is not sufficient to fulfill the requirements of their position as leaders; women frequently undergo self-initiative-based training that does not follow a strategic plan for organizational leadership development (Al-Ahmadi, 2005).

In this part, some previous studies that focused on issues and challenges facing Saudi working women have been reviewed, as this issue is considered one of the sensitive issues that must be addressed in Saudi society. Previous studies have shown that there is gender discrimination in Saudi society, so we find differences in dealing with Employees and bias towards male employees. In Saudi society, Individuals have a narrow view of women and it would appear that gender roles do not encourage women to enjoy their rights. Those barriers were supposed to face Saudi women. Saudi women must break free from the gender roles that the culture places on them in the guise of religion.

Femininity versus masculinity

There is a marked lack of mentoring services to promote the development of women's careers in the Arab context. Women tend to be more distant from their male counterparts, who also monitor critical organizational data. Additionally, female employees also depend on their families to sustain their employment (Abalkhail, 2012; Al-Ahmadi, 2011; Al-Lamki, 1999; Jamali, Sidani, and Safieddine, 2005; Tlaiss and Kauser, 2010, 2011a). Tlaiss and Kauser (2011a) note that this statement means that having help from their male family members (usually their husband or father) is crucial for women. Women often appear to draw support from other close family ties (wasta), which have allowed them to gain non-executive roles in organizations (Tlaiss and Kauser, 2011a; Singh, 2008).

In encouraging and motivating women to gain success in the workplace, male family members and their connections play an important role. While it can be argued that Arab women have strong unity in such a way that their own informal networks play a significant role in empowering them in the public sphere, it is significant to mention that female networks are also connected to male networks (Abalkhail, 2012; Metcalfe, 2006). Therefore, Arab women may find it difficult to maintain knowledge and insights without the assistance of powerful family members, in particular male relations.

Nevertheless, it is inequitable to improve women's employment such that they gain access to senior roles in institutions by depending only on family support. There are not all women with loving families or close family relations. Consequently, in organizations, as well as in society and governments, HRD departments need to play a significant role in developing strategies and initiatives to enable women and men to achieve true equality and to gain equal opportunities to leadership roles. The advancement of women's careers must be incorporated into institutional HRD strategies and approaches, including preparation, mentoring, and access to knowledge and networks in leadership development programs (Burke, 2002).

Generally, the idea of leadership has been correlated with male behaviors and attributes like strength, dominance, and assertiveness (Alomiri, 2015). While there is no proof that such qualities are correlated with actual leadership, it seems that they have been socially and culturally. Although there are several instances of women, leaders in Islamic literature, over the past century, Saudi women have traditionally faced cultural and conventional gender bias, not just in the context of leadership, but also in all areas of life. Females are absent from public life in Saudi Arabia (Alotaibi, 2020).

According to researchers (Al-Ahmadi, 2011; Alsuwaida, 2016; Al-Kayed, 2015), due to gender bias, female leaders lack opportunities and feel helpless. Much research has implications for the production of leadership to resolve women's empowerment problems. Al-Shaalan and Kaki (2013), quoted in Al Ghamdi (2016), found that in Saudi universities, there are obstacles to the empowerment process for women that influence the quality of the performance of the manufacturing university. These include excessive centralization, the predominance of employee jobs, work schedules, management traditions, lack of decision-making interaction, and low staff productivity (Al Ghamdi, 2016).

Summary

The second chapter focused on literature and previous studies that are related to the topic of the current study. In this chapter, the researcher tried to cover all the literature related to the concept of Saudi women, the empowerment of Saudi women, their role in society, and the factors that affect their access to non-traditional jobs.

We also discussed the view of Islam towards women. Although Islam honors women, some misunderstand Islam regarding women through strictness and restriction on women, locking them up at home and making their primary job a housewife.

This chapter also focused on the past and present of the Kingdom of Saudi Arabia. In the past few years, society's view of women has changed, and it has allowed them to obtain many of their rights, such as employment, entry into cinemas, driving vehicles, obtaining leadership positions, and so on. The Saudi government has paid great attention to women in recent years, as the Kingdom's Vision 2030 has included many principles that promote women's empowerment. Despite the government's interest in Saudi women, Saudi women still suffer from many challenges and obstacles that affect their access to new non-traditional jobs and leadership positions in institutions.

This chapter included the challenges and obstacles that Saudi women face in the work environment, such as gender bias, marginalization, marital status, and so on. In the past time, a small but growing strand of research related to women's professions and, more specifically, women in management and leadership has developed from the Middle East. This entails, for instance: Bahrain (Metcalfe, 2006, 2007); Lebanon (Sidani et al . , 2015; Tlaiss, 2014; Tlaiss and Dirani, 2015); Saudi Arabia, Kuwait and the UAE (Abalkhail and Allan, 2016); Jordan and Oman (Metcalfe, 2006); and Middle East comparative studies (Metcalfe 2008). These latest studies illustrate a broad range of factors important to recognizing the under-representation of women in the country's leadership (and the workplace).

In particular, Metcalfe's joint research (2006, 2007, 2008, 2011) and Kauser and Tlaiss' systematic analysis (2011) highlight cultural patterns that direct definitions of the right of women to work and establish expectations of gender roles. In specific, Research indicates that conventional gender hierarchies and patriarchal organizational systems favor men by offering access to substantial networks of individuals and families (Metcalfe, 2007). That is not to suggest that women cannot profit from Wasta, which means 'a social network of interpersonal relations, rooted in links of family and kinship' (Abalkhail and Allan, 2016, p. 162). Indeed, this can provide women with contacts to obtain career opportunities, and it is the best way to gain professional effect; but women should rely specifically on male family members to promote broader social contacts (Doumato, 2010). Male leadership characteristics thrive within patriarchal systems, while women suffer from age-old gender roles that perceive women as better suited to positions as mothers and wives (Sidani et al., 2015).

Chapter 3: Methodology

Introduction

The literature review constituted the research problem and paved the way for the study

direction. The purpose of this qualitative study was to investigate the challenges and issues that

Saudi women face when appointed to new unconventional jobs. Once the problem was identified

and understood from the context of the living experience of previous researchers, potential

factors and challenges were identified that affect the appointment of Saudi women to new, non-

traditional positions from a scientific perspective. Doing so paves the way for subsequent

research to address the challenges and issues Saudi women face when they are appointed to new,

unconventional jobs, thus enhancing the empowerment of Saudi women, and reducing the gender

gap and gender bias in Saudi society.

Exploring the challenges and issues affecting Saudi women's work is in line with the use

of phenomena as a methodology for qualitative research. The transcendent phenomena made it

possible to focus on the essence of the experience and to crystallize the challenges and basic

issues of non-traditional jobs for Saudi women. The research questions that guided the study,

based on the main objectives, enabled the participants to share various aspects of their

experiences and perceptions related to the topic of the study. The nature and scope of the

narrative questions allowed the participants to recount their experiences in a way that respected

their opinions and perspectives related to the study questions.

The purpose of this chapter is to demarcate this research's methodological approach. The

chapter will clarify and justify the approach selected to perform this analysis. In this part, the

procedures followed during the analysis are included. It presents a full overview of the study

methods, the population, the sample, the methods for collecting data, the pilot analysis, the program overview used in the analysis, and the nature of the research. In addition, it presents the statistical techniques used during the analysis.

The Study Approach

According to Creswell (2008) and Merriam (2002), the problem investigated plays an important role in choosing the method of analysis. A qualitative inquiry was selected as the most effective methodological approach to address the research questions of this study. The purpose of the qualitative study is to understand the socially created meaning for people as they communicate with the community (Merriam, 2002). Thus, the focus of this study was on the perceptions of women, how they viewed the world, and how they perceived their lives and made sense of them (Merriam, 2002). Merriam (2002) said, "Questions of context, interpretation, and method are suitable for a qualitative study" (Merriam, 2002, p. 19). Because this qualitative study attempt to understand Saudi women's stories about their experiences in achieving roles in new unconventional work, and their anticipated social function and gender norms, the best approach was a narrative inquiry.

To achieve the research goals and to address the research problem that revolves around the challenges and issues facing Saudi women working in sensitive positions such as aviation, art, engineering and architecture, a descriptive-analytical approach and qualitative research methods as interviews will be used. Several personal interviews will be conducted with a number of Saudi women working in sensitive positions and discussion many issues they faced before and during the current position.

Data Collection

Often, data in scientific studies and research are classified into two types, which are primary data and secondary data, and these two types differ in the methods and ways in which they are collected.

- **Primary data:** In this study, will be collected through an interviews with Saudi women employed in new unconventional jobs in the Kingdom of Saudi Arabia.

The following procedural steps were implemented to conduct this case study. First, some prospective participants known to the researcher were called or emailed and invited to participate in the study. The email included information about the researcher and the study to establish rapport. In addition, other acquaintances working in higher education were asked for assistance in identifying and suggesting names of Saudi female leaders who might be interested in participating. After receiving the suggested names and information, these female leaders were contacted via email and invited to participate in the study. Next, a convenient time and place was arranged for the interview according to the participants' preference and schedule.

- **Secondary data:** will be collected through a theoretical and systematic review of previous studies, research, literature, journals, and books related to the subject of the current study.

Qualitative Research

Qualitative approaches show a distinct approach to the scholarly investigation than quantitative analytical techniques. Although the processes are identical, qualitative approaches depend on data from text and pictures, have specific data analysis steps, and draw on different designs. To write a methodology section for a qualitative research proposal partly involves educating readers on the intent of qualitative research, mentioning designs, carefully reflecting on the role of the researcher in the analysis, drawing on an ever-expanding list of types of data sources, utilizing specific data recording protocols, analyzing the data through multiple steps of an information (Creswell & Creswell, 2017).

Qualitative research aims to "illustrate the meanings and behaviors that people make and to include explanations of how and why" (Luttrell, 2010, p. 1). Because of the sensitivity and durability of approaches, it can gain significant insights into how people live or perceive their lives. Denzin and Lincoln (2003, p. 4) note that: "Qualitative research is a positioned practice in the environment that locates the observer". Qualitative research takes place in natural environments and attempts to understand their experiences through the eyes of the participants (Creswell, 2009).

To gain a strong, thorough understanding of a phenomenon, qualitative methodologies are correlated with interpretative approaches. Therefore, it reflects on utilizing terms in the compilation and analysis of data, rather than quantification (Bryman, 2016). In order to answer questions and to investigate humans in their natural environments, qualitative research depends on verbal and visual communication (Lichtman, 2013), and may involve analyzing photographs or objects (Punch and Oancea, 2014). qualitative methodologies are solid in those areas which have been described as possible vulnerabilities within the quantitative methodology. Gray (2014:34) nevertheless, reminds us "generalizability is less important in qualitative research than understanding the actual operations behind the fact."

The numbers and styles of approaches have also become more clear since the 1990s and into the 21st century in qualitative research. Anthropology, sociology, humanities, and assessment derived from the historical roots of the qualitative study. Books also described the

34

different forms, and unique qualitative investigative methods are now available for full procedures (Clandinin and Connelly, 2000).

The philosophical principles and processes of the phenomenological approach were explored by Moustakas (1994); the procedures of grounded theory were defined by Charmaz (2006), Corbin and Strauss (2007), and Strauss and Corbin (1990, 1998). Fetterman (2010) and Wolcott (2008), and Stake (1995) have described ethnographic techniques and the various faces and analysis methods of ethnography and Yin (2009, 2012) have proposed complexities occurring in case study research. The following techniques are illustrated, understanding that methods including participatory action study (Kemmis & McTaggart, 2000), discourse analysis (Cheek, 2004), and others not listed are also viable ways of conducting qualitative studies:

- Narrative research is a humanities research model in which the researcher examines people's lives and asks one or more people to provide stories about their lives (Riessman, 2008). This knowledge is then also retold into a narrative chronology by the researcher or restored. In the end, the narrative also incorporates experiences from the life of the participant with those from the life of the researcher in a shared narrative (Clandinin & Connelly, 2000).

- The phenomenological study is a model of research that comes from philosophy and psychology in which the researcher explains individuals' lived perceptions of a phenomenon as defined by participants. The nature of the experiences of many people who have all witnessed the phenomenon culminates in this definition. This design has solid conceptual roots and generally requires interviews (Giorgi, 2009; Moustakas, 1994).

"Phenomenology" arose from the term "phainómenon" in ancient Greek, which means "things that appear to be seen." It is the study of conscious experiences from the point of view of the first person (Gallagher, 2012). As a technique, it is typically a qualitative approach that focuses on the details of their perceptions of the array of study participants.

Centered on a descriptive phenomenological approach, the method of thematic analysis goes from the original data to the recognition of meanings, arranging them into patterns and writing down the effects of the topics relevant to the purpose of the research and the real context. These are represented conversely when the results are published (i.e., starting with the themes and the descriptive text, illustrated with quotes). Therefore, meanings derived from the experiences of participants are represented in a meaningful text structured into themes (Sundler et al, 2019).

- Grounded theory is a sociological study design in which the researcher derives a common, abstract theory based on the views of participants of a process, behavior, or interaction. This method includes the use of several data collection stages and the refining and interrelation of knowledge categories (Charmaz, 2006; Corbin & Strauss, 2007).

- Ethnography is a study design derived from anthropology and sociology in which the researcher examines, over a long period of time, the shared patterns of attitudes, vocabulary, and acts of an intact cultural community in a natural environment. Observations and interviews also require data collection.

- **Case studies** are a model of research used in several fields, particularly assessment, in which the researcher performs an in-depth analysis of a case, often a system, occurrence, behavior, procedure, or one or more persons. Cases are constrained by time and operation, and researchers gather extensive information over a prolonged period using a range of data collection methods (Stake, 1995; Yin, 2009; Yin, 2012).

Case Study Data Collection

The current research will take the last form of qualitative research, which is the case study research model that is compatible with the nature of the study and its variables, by focusing on the career and family lives of the participants and discussing their experiences and the challenges they faced during their work in new non-traditional jobs.

In their real-life contexts, the case study approach allows for in-depth, multi-faceted analysis of complex problems. Usually, information is obtained from a variety of sources and using many various methodologies (for instance observations & interviews). The data is predominantly biographical and relates to events in the history (for example retrospective) of the person, including important events currently occurring in his or her daily life (Crowe et al., 2011).

Yin (2009, p. 19), a recognized pioneer in case study methodology, stressed that case studies can also be useful for describing presumed causal connections "too complex" for the study or experimental designs between variables (for example, treatment and intervention results). In addition, where findings are not explicit, they can explain the real-life context in a causal chain, demonstrate particular structures, and illuminate a situation. In case study design, theoretical ideas are important and are generally created prior to data collection since they direct the form of data collected. These can be "stories" that relate events in a process or define characteristics and skills in a systemic context and are instrumental in describing complex outcomes (Suter, 2012).

Depending on the epistemological point of view of the researcher, case studies can be approached in various ways, that is, whether they take a critical (questioning the conclusions of one's own and others), interpretive (trying to understand individual and shared social meanings) or positivist approach (oriented towards natural science standards, like concentrating on generalizability considerations) (Doolin, 1998).

In the current study, special emphasis will be placed on the interpretive and the positivist approach, where the participants' responses and actions will be interpreted during the interview, and then an attempt will be made to develop generalizable considerations.

The case study methodology is well suited to collecting data on more explanatory 'how',' what' and 'why' issues, like 'how is the intervention being carried out and collected on the ground? '. The case study approach will provide more insights into what weaknesses remain in its execution or why one implementation technique can be selected over another (Pearson et al, 2010). The researcher developed 13 personal interview questions applicable to create a high-quality case study, which are: (1) how old are you?; (2) What is your current job?; (3) Why did you choose this job?; (4) Did you receive any support or assistance from family and friends?; (5) In your opinion, what is the role of the family in supporting and assistance Saudi women working in new non-traditional jobs?; (6) What are the motivations and advantages that you have seen in this work?; (7) Do you have any reservations about your work?; (8) What problems and challenges did you face?; (9) How were these problems affecting you?; (10) What possible solutions have you thought of?; (11) What would have happened if you had not accepted this job?; (12) Have you thought about the risks before accepting the job? What are these risks?; (13) In your opinion, do working Saudi women have a role in the cultural and economic development of society? How?

Semi-structured interviews

Interviews are the primary instrument for qualitative analysis. In co-creating awareness, they play a crucial role (Hand, 2003). Interviews are described by Ritchie and Lewis (2003) and Gillham (2000) as a controlled verbal exchange, whose usefulness is profoundly dependent on the "interviewer's social skills" (Clough & Nutbrown, 2007). These skills can include the ability to clearly structure questions (Cohen et al., 2007); listen respectfully and carefully (Clough & Nutbrown, 2007); enable interviewees to speak, and openly convey "make it easy to respond to interviewees" (Clough & Nutbrown, 2007, p. 134).

Three key forms of interviews are available: structured, unstructured, and semi-structured. Each has its own criterion and the particular form selected depending on the objectives and questions of the study. The respondent is asked a series of closed questions in standardized interviews and all respondents will be asked the same questions in the same order. The interviewer (Wellington, 2015) directs a formal interview. These are like questionnaires whose highly structured nature can impede respondents' ability to provide illuminating data in a way that they want (Gray, 2014).

Unstructured interviews are in-depth investigations of the perspectives and interpretations of the interviewees in their own words (Punch and Oancea, 2014). Unstructured interviews rely heavily on interviewer's socialization skills (Wellington, 2015), which should ensure that the interviewees remain concentrated on research problems (Basit, 2010). In academic research, semi-structured interviews are the most preferred form of the interview. Patten (2016) indicates that the merits of the approach make it appealing, while semi-structured personal interviews create content that can take time to understand.

In this study, semi-structured interviews were the main means of data collection. "Semi-structured interviews consist of predetermined questions relating to domains of interest, administered to a representative sample of respondents to validate domains of the research, and define causes, variables, and variables' items or attributes for review or use in the survey" (Schensul, 1999, p. 149 On both practical and ethical grounds, the researcher preferred semi-structured interviews. Since this study was aimed at examining how Saudi women could be motivated by Saudi women, required an approach that would allow participants to explain the challenges and issues that Saudi women face when they are assigned to high, new, and challenging positions. This methodology is considered one of the favored feminist research methodologies (DeVault & Gross, 2007). Therefore, considering the nature of this study, semi-structured interviews were an acceptable approach.

Moreover, interviews put importance on personal language as data. Face-to-face interviews can be sufficient if the depth of context is necessary and the study focuses mainly on obtaining insight and understanding (Gillham, 2000, p. 11; Ritchie & Lewis, 2003, p. 138). Therefore, using this approach offered adequate space for the interviewees to convey and provide examples of their daily working lives, and to follow up on and discuss any new problems that were presented. With the use of questionnaires or formal interviews, this could not have been achieved because the formal style of these approaches would not have allowed to follow up on new issues that arose.

There are many ways of conducting interviews that allow video conferencing: face-to-face, by phone or using digital communication, like email or web applications. More lately, technology has allowed online face-to-face interviews for respondents (Weller, 2017), but physical face-to-face interviews are still preferred. In addition, in cases where interviewees have restricted access to the internet, the former approach raises difficulties.

Online interviews are easy; they have many of the same benefits of face-to-face interviews, but they appear to be shorter and lack sensory stimuli of face-to-face interviews (Cohen et al., 2011). They need careful scheduling and period plans (Oppenheim, 1992), but are acceptable when it is difficult to meet face-to-face. Generally, they are based on the same kinds of questions as those in questionnaires, making them easier to tabulate (Patten, 2016), while questions that require specific responses are often asked and can be audio documented with the approval of the interviewees. They can be used to gather sensitive information, or where "some confidentiality is needed" (Opdenakker, 2006:11). Another benefit is that it is often easier for respondents to meet those (Cohen et al., 2011) and no time is wasted on driving. The key drawback of telephone interviews is that, while social signals like voice and intonation are still usable, body language cannot be used as a source of additional knowledge (Opdenakker, 2006). Furthermore, participants should actually "hang up on the caller" (Cohen et al., 2011:275).

In this study, the interviews were conducted online through the internet (due to the conditions that the world is witnessing in light of the spread of the new Corona virus), where the respondents were contacted and the appropriate time for them to conduct the interview remotely. The researcher also convinced the participants of the importance of operating the camera so that the interviews would be closer to face-to-face interviews and so that the researcher could notice all the details he needed.

The Population of the Study

Reid (2013) identified the population as all groups with certain features that are of significance to researchers' research. The population can be interpreted from the concept as the intended community or group of people involved or chosen by the researcher for the study (Reid, 2013). The population of the study consisted of all Saudi women working in new unconventional jobs.

The Sample of the Study

According to Cohen et al. (2011), Sampling is the process of choosing a small group from a larger group to concentrate on. This is important since it can be expensive and time-consuming to perform research with large populations. All participants who met the requirements for inclusion in the research were included in the population (Sani, 2018). The researcher works with a sample almost always (Gorard, 2003), where the word sample is used to denote a smaller group, which is typically a population-representative, but not always (Oppenheim, 1992). Sampling has the advantage of making it simpler for the category in question to be tested. The sample size, nevertheless, relies on the population's heterogeneity or homogeneity, and the sampling technique must be suitable for the analysis. in general, the larger the sample, the best for quantitative research, as it offers greater reliability (Cohen et al., 2011), while samples are generally small for practical reasons like costs and time to produce and interpret data in qualitative research. The survey should provide access to adequate data in both cases with the right emphasis to allow the research questions to be dealt with.

In order to survey the opinion of Saudi women working in different fields about the challenges and issues that Saudi women face when they are appointed to these jobs, the researcher decided to achieve career diversity in selecting participants, so that women working in different fields are chosen, thus achieving career diversity. The researcher was also keen on selecting participants from different age groups to achieve diversity in age groups as well. Therefore, an intended sample was chosen Out of 10 Saudi women work in new non-traditional jobs. They were searched through social media platforms such as Twitter and LinkedIn and communicated with them electronically via the Zoom platform, where they searched for Saudi women with non-traditional professions (such as a plane captain, executive director, sales representative, driving trainer, female soldier, or player or football coach or other Sports) and their consent to participate in this study will be taken.

Ethical Consideration

According to the Ethical Guidelines for Educational Research (BERA, 2011), an expansion of the awareness of institutional knowledge is the aim of researchers within education. In addition, any educational study should be carried out ethically, it has been asserted. This is why the researcher claims that upholding and following ethical standards in this dissertation was important. Therefore, in the study, the researcher requires ethical consent from the participants. Participants will also be told about the study and what it aims to achieve.

According to BERA (2011), all studies on the handling and use of personal data should comply with legal requirements, such as the Data Protection Act (1998). Before the disclosure of their character details to third parties, the investigator will request permission from the participants. Consequently, their identity will be kept confidential in this research to ensure that they are empowered to give their honest opinion. The confidentiality and privacy of the participant's personal data will be emphasized, and it is emphasized that this information will only be used for scientific research and development purposes.

Regarding the right to withdraw, participants will be told that without needing to give any explanations, they have the right to withdraw from the study (BERA, 2011). After trying, with care, to convince them to participate again, the decision to withdraw will be approved by the participant's will. Participants can suffer discomfort or irritation during the research process, according to BERA (2011). Therefore, to deal with the causes of emotional distress, the researcher will take the necessary steps. In addition, Ethical Research Involving Children (ERIC) calls for proper consideration for children's interests, integrity, and welfare (Powell et al., 2011).

In addition, the participants were fill in the Roehampton ethics application form before the dissertation begins. This was being driven by ethical instructions and applied. These ethical guidelines are intended to contribute to making the research more successful by ensuring that all stakeholders' interests are maintained in the study.

Summary

In this chapter, the methodology used for the study was discussed, including the population selection process, survey design, data collection procedures, and data analysis. In addition, details about the essence of the interview that was intended for the study was presented. The chapter also outlined the significance and ethical concerns of human subjects.

In this study, case study qualitative research methods were chosen, and to collect qualitative data for the study, the semi-structured interview tool was used, which allowed the researcher to pose questions that led to in-depth responses, to prove responses from the interview data, and to allow interviewees to inform my research with more ideas that address Research questions. The researcher took into account the need to allow the interviewees to express their feelings and views while maintaining a degree of control over the conduct of the interviews. Moreover, the researcher considered that data analysis and interpretation of 10 semi-structured interviews could have been managed and that the data would enrich his current study because the interviews focused on specific topics.

Chapter 4: Data Analysis and Discussion

Introduction

The aim of this research is to investigate the challenges and issues faced by Saudi women when they are appointed to new unconventional jobs. The research is based on a series of semi-structured interviews with a range of participants: Saudi women who work in new unconventional jobs.

The key findings of the study are presented in this chapter, which were extracted from data collected from 10 Saudi women working in new unconventional jobs. The interviewees' answers to the semi-structured questions asked in the interviews are recorded in this chapter. Through first posing the interview questions and then discussing the answers from the lecturers and Academic Development Practitioners, the researcher works through the interview questions in a structured manner. The results of the interviews are then accompanied by concrete findings. The researcher aims to summarize the overall results from these interviews in the final discussion of this chapter.

Each interview transcript was analyzed in two phases. First, the transcripts were translated into English, and the translations were reviewed to ensure their accuracy. Second, the transcripts were read repeatedly to code the data and identify relevant themes. Under the thematic analysis approach, the interviews were systematically coded and recoded paying attention to details about challenges and issues faced by Saudi women when they are appointed to new unconventional jobs. Content analysis based on the frequency of occurrence of themes was performed to identify recurring themes which emerged from the data.

The data analysis and results of this study are presented and discussed in depth in this chapter. Results are presented in terms of demographic and social factors. Participants' responses to semi-structured interview questions are also documented in this chapter. The researcher takes a structured approach to interview questions, first asking them and then discussing the participants' answers.

Interviews Distribution

This chapter attempts to analyze the data collected from semi-structured face-to-face interviews conducted with a sample of (10) Saudi women working in new unconventional jobs. The purpose is to examine and interpret the responses of the interviewed participants to the interview questions in order to obtain the required information that ends with an exploration of the main findings and formulation of the conceptual perspective in order to arrive at appropriate recommendations and suggestions regarding the topic of the study.

The purpose of illustrating the analysis of data and results is to provide a clear understanding of the challenges and issues that Saudi women face when assigned to new unconventional jobs. Interviews were conducted with a sample of Saudi women working in new, non-traditional jobs. Therefore, both explanations and quotes from those interviewed were provided to illustrate the study results. Sandelowski (2010) stated that showing citations with descriptions and explanations encourages readers to engage with the interviewees' thoughts and deeply understand their perspectives. Accordingly, Sandelowski's concept of objective qualitative content analysis is followed; Taking, encoding, and grouping important data sets according to themes, each subject conveys a different unit of information.

Interviews were coded and presented in the form of themes to answer the research questions, and the coding framework was developed in a way that allows this. The coding includes coding patterns and themes in such a way to give greater clarity regarding their detailed content. To do this, a distinction was made between the different aspects of the content by organizing data into a group of categories; dividing the questions and their answers into groups (topics) that answer the questions of the study.

The interview guide consisted of two main parts with a different number of open questions that gave the respondent the freedom to express his or her opinion/words. The first part of the interview is a part that does not serve any of the aims of the study but is merely a description of the study sample and its demographic characteristics. The second part of the interview consisted of 12 questions mainly directed to identify the challenges and issues faced by Saudi women when they are appointed to new unconventional jobs.

Respondent's Demographic Background

Ten Saudi women working in new, non-traditional jobs were interviewed individually for approximately 30 minutes and no more than an hour during this study. The age groups of the participants varied, as there were two participants from the age group less than 30, 4 participants from the age group 31-40, 3 participants from the age group 41-50 and one female from the age group over 50, and this was represented in figure 1.

All interviewees are 2 females and 4 males, who are between 26 and 55 years old and have experience in different fields such as construction and architectural design and this allowed a wide range of responses to be obtained that are compatible with the problem of the current study. It also ensures that some answers resulted from awareness and the experience of those in the interior field.

The detailed demographic profiles of those interviewees are as shown in the following charts:

Figure 1

Age of respondents

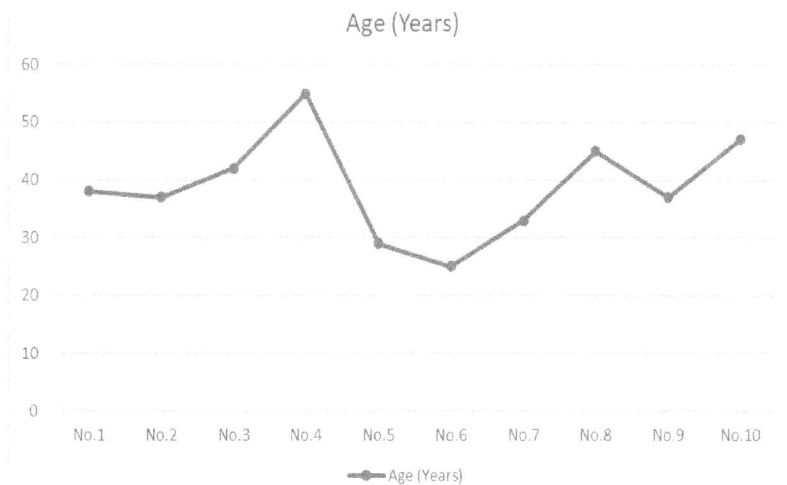
Age (Years)

The marital status of the participants varied, as some of the participants were unmarried, married,

widowed, or divorced. The ratios were represented as follows:

Figure 2

Marital status of respondents

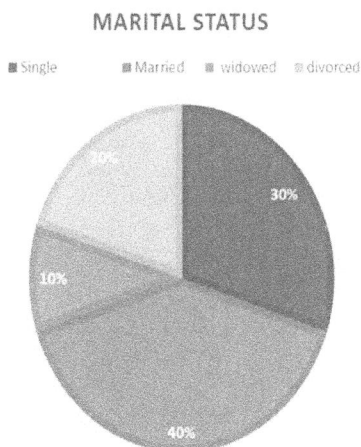
MARITAL STATUS

There was a difference in the years of experience the participants had. This was represented as follows:

Figure 3

Years of experience

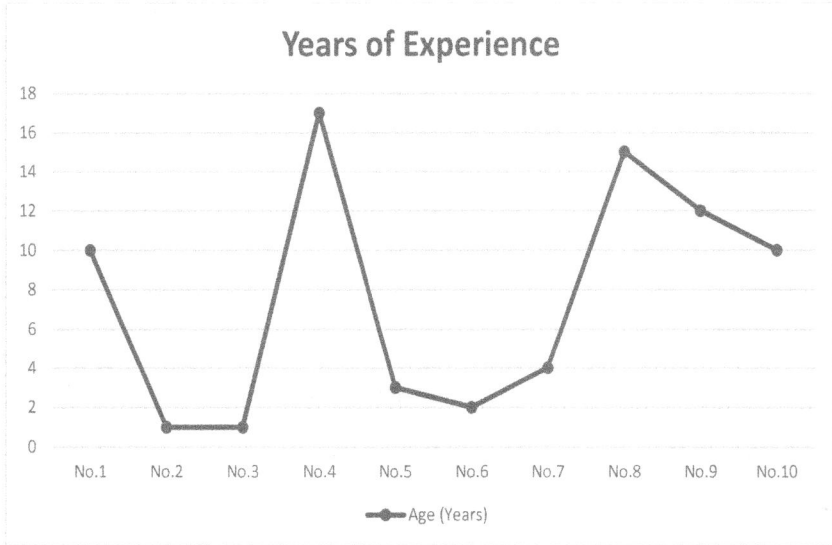

In addition, the Qualifications and educational level of the participants was different, and it was relatively represented as follows:

Figure 4

Qualifications of res²ⁿᵗˢ

QUALIFICATIONS

■ High S   icate   ■ Bachelor's Degree   ■ Master's Degree   ■ Doctoral Degree

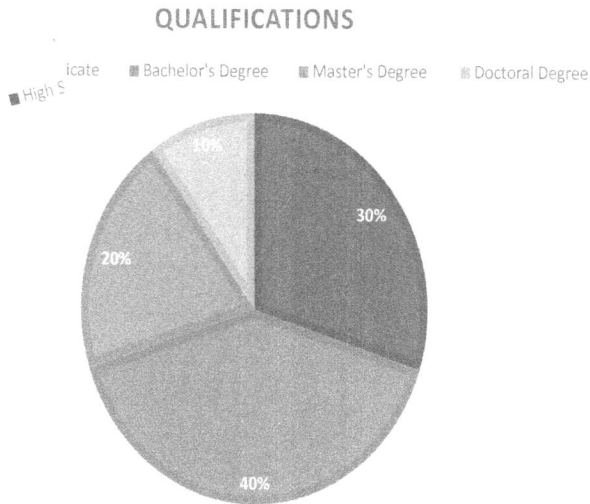

Presentation of the semi-structured interview data

ion 1: *What is your current job?*

...ve the main objective of this study, which is to discuss the challenges and issues

...ien face when they are appointed to new non-traditional jobs, the researcher asked

...stions related to this topic, where the first question was to inquire about the

...ents' work field and their jobs.

Regarding the responses of the interviewees to the first question, the respondents were

mployees in many fields and sectors, the most important of which are medicine, engineering,

car driver (Uber captain), Driving instructor, CEO, Security guard in a mall, Female police

officer, and Sales employee in a cosmetic store. For the detailed responses, see Table below. The

results obtained through the respondents' answers to the first question indicate that the Kingdom

Figure 4

Qualifications of respondents

QUALIFICATIONS

■ High School Certificate　　■ Bachelor's Degree　　■ Master's Degree　　■ Doctoral Degree

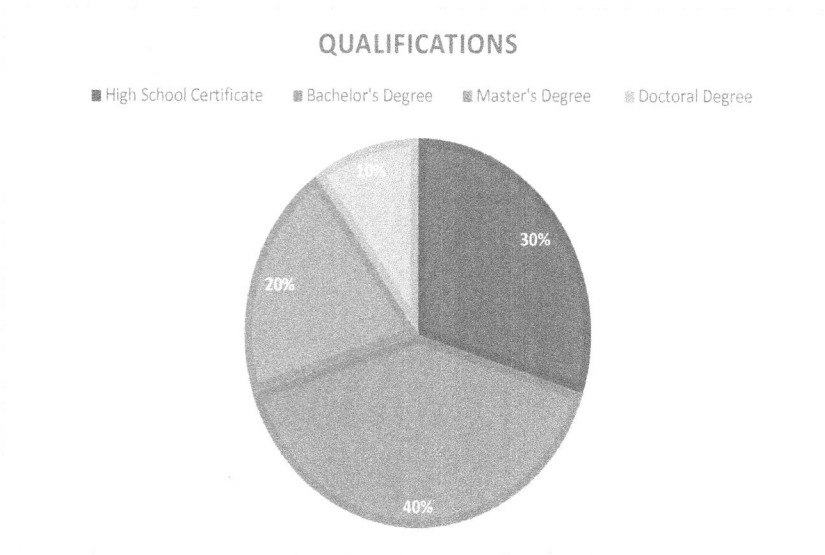

Presentation of the semi-structured interview data

- ***Question 1:*** *What is your current job?*

To achieve the main objective of this study, which is to discuss the challenges and issues that Saudi women face when they are appointed to new non-traditional jobs, the researcher asked a set of questions related to this topic, where the first question was to inquire about the respondents' work field and their jobs.

Regarding the responses of the interviewees to the first question, the respondents were employees in many fields and sectors, the most important of which are medicine, engineering, car driver (Uber captain), Driving instructor, CEO, Security guard in a mall, Female police officer, and Sales employee in a cosmetic store. For the detailed responses, see Table below. The results obtained through the respondents' answers to the first question indicate that the Kingdom of Saudi Arabia seeks to empower women and integrate them into the labor market in various fields, which is consistent with what was stated in the Alfarran (2016), which emphasized the increase in women's participation in the labor market in Saudi Arabia during the past years.

Table 1

Interviewees' responses to a question about the respondents' current job

Interviewee No.	Response
Interviewee No.1	Engineer
Interviewee No.2	Car Driver (Captain Uber)
Interviewee No.3	Driving instructor
Interviewee No.4	Executive Director
Interviewee No.5	Security guard in a mall
Interviewee No.6	Sales employee in a cosmetic store
Interviewee No.7	Women's hairdresser
Interviewee No.8	A teacher and a lecturer at university
Interviewee No.9	Female police officer
Interviewee No.10	doctor gynecologist

- *Question 2: Why did you choose this job?*

In the same context, the researcher asked the respondents a question to discuss their reasons for choosing these jobs. The reasons for choosing these jobs varied. The interviewee No. (1) Stated: "*I chose this job because it is in my field of study and scientific experience.*" This is consistent with what the interviewee No. (10) Said, who also indicated that she chose this job because of her passion and love for this field, said: "*My childhood ambition has been to become a doctor who treats people. I always persevered and worked hard to achieve my dream of becoming a doctor, and thank God, I achieved that*".This agrees with the responses of respondents No. (7), respondents No. (3) and Respondent No. (9).

It is clear from the answers of the ten Saudi women interviewed that there are some common reasons that prompted them to choose their current occupations. The most prominent of these reasons was that these jobs are related to the respondents' field of study, or the respondents' passion and desire to work in this field. However, interviewee No. (5) indicated that she accepted the job so that she could help her family cover the financial obligations, said, "I accepted this job so that I could help my husband cover the household obligations."

In addition, for the remainder of the interviewees' answers, the following table shows detailed interview answers regarding the respondents' reasons for choosing current jobs.

Table 2

Interviewees' responses to a question about why respondents chose the current job

Interviewee No.	Response
Interviewee No.1	I chose this position because it is in my field of study and scientific experience.
Interviewee No.2	After King Salman bin Abdulaziz, may God protect him, ordered the decision to allow Saudi women to drive, I went to the transport company as an experiment, and after that, I started working and delivering passengers.
Interviewee No.3	I chose this job because I love to drive cars, I learned to drive cars when I was residing outside the Kingdom. In addition, when the law allowing Saudi women to drive was issued, I felt it was my duty to share my driving experience with Saudi women so that they could drive.
Interviewee No.4	I did not choose this job, but I gradually got it through the job hierarchy and my efficiency at work.
Interviewee No.5	I accepted this job so that I could help my husband cover the household obligations.
Interviewee No.6	I love cosmetics, skincare, and beauty and this is what encouraged me to accept this job as it is related to the field of cosmetics and beauty.
Interviewee No.7	Since my childhood, I have been interested in hair care and styling, and with time I learned how to cut and style hair with high skill, and

	then I entered the labor market by establishing a beauty center where I work.
Interviewee No.8	In the beginning, I worked as a teacher in a females' school, and because of my love for science and study, I completed higher educations and graduated with a High Distinction (HD), which provided me with a job as a lecturer at the university.
Interviewee No.9	I chose this profession because I love leadership work, helping the weak, fairness of rights, and applying the law to everyone.
Interviewee No.10	My childhood ambition has been to become a doctor who treats people. I always persevered and worked hard to achieve my dream of becoming a doctor, and thank God, I achieved that.

- ***Question 3:*** *Did you receive any support or assistance from family and friends?*

In order to obtain details about the role of the family in supporting and assisting Saudi women working in new non-traditional jobs, the researcher asked the respondents about the extent to which they received any support or assistance from family and friends. The responses of the participants were divided into two answers, the first: Yes, she received support and help from the family, and this applies to respondent No. (7), who said: "*Of course, I certainly received financial and moral support from my family. My father is the one who takes care of all the expenses of the beauty center and he always asks me if I need any support*". As well as Participant No. (8), who also confirmed that she received support from her family, especially her mother and husband; said: "*I definitely got the support of my family and husband. They always encourage me to study and help me complete some household tasks so that I can devote myself to studying, especially during exams, as my husband does almost all the housework and takes care of the children, and provides me with a suitable environment for study.*"

On the other hand, the responses of some respondents indicated that they did not receive any support from family and friends, especially family. The family's reaction was total opposition to accepting this job, but with the respondents' insistence on working, their families agreed to their work. Interview No. (2) indicated that her family was strongly opposed to her accepting her current job, and said: "*to be frank, my family strongly opposed this, especially since allowing women to drive in Saudi Arabia is a new decision and was not recognized before, but because of my insistence on this profession and their belief that I would not be able to continue in this profession, they agreed to that.*" The same applies to Interview No. (6), which confirmed that her family did not support her at first and were opposed to her accepting her current job, and the interviewee said: "*At first, they did not accept it, Women's work was rejected in our families and Saudi society, and I had great difficulty in convincing them.*"

For the rest of the respondent's answers, the following table shows the answers of all the women interviewed regarding the extent to which they received support and assistance from family and friends.

Table 3

Interviewees' responses to a question about the extent to which they received any support or assistance from family and friends

Interviewee No.	Response
Interviewee No.1	Yes, I received support from my family, as they were the first who supported me and encouraged me to enter this specialization, and they did not object to my acceptance of this job. However, they had some apprehension about the work environment and co-workers.
Interviewee No.2	To be frank, my family strongly opposed this, especially since allowing women to drive in Saudi Arabia is a new decision and was not recognized before, but because of my insistence on this profession and their belief that I would not be able to continue in this profession, they agreed to that.
Interviewee No.3	Yes, I have had great support from my family, they are always the first supporter for me to work.
Interviewee No.4	Certainly, the family is the first supporter for me and my husband, may God protect him, always loves to see me in the highest positions, and is always proud of me.

Interviewee No.5	In fact, my family did not want me to accept this job, but because of the bad financial conditions and their need for financial support, I managed to convince them of the job.
Interviewee No.6	At first, they did not accept it, Women's work was rejected in our families and Saudi society, and I had great difficulty in convincing them.
Interviewee No.7	Of course, I certainly received financial and moral support from my family. My father is the one who takes care of all the expenses of the beauty center and he always asks me if I need any support.
Interviewee No.8	I definitely got the support of my family and husband. They always encourage me to study and help me complete some household tasks so that I can devote myself to studying, especially during exams, as my husband does almost all the housework and takes care of the children, and provides me with a suitable environment for study.
Interviewee No.9	My family's views were different. My mother strongly refused and said to me who will marry you while you work in a manly job, but my father was always supportive and encouraged me to do what I always love, but he always reminded me of the dangers of this job and asked me whether you would be able to face these risks.
Interviewee No.10	Of course, I definitely got the support of my family, especially my mother and husband. My mother always takes care of my children and my husband is always by my side, especially when I am called to the hospital at night.

The participants' responses to this question confirm that Saudi society is still not accepting of the idea of Saudi women working and engaging in the labor market. This is consistent with the findings of Swaantje (2018), which showed that Saudi society presents an interesting paradox with regard to female participation in the labor market. Despite higher living standards and education levels among women, Saudi society has the largest gender employment gap in the world.

- *Question 4: In your opinion, what is the role of the family in supporting and assistance Saudi women working in new unconventional jobs?*

In this context, the researcher also raised another question centered on the role of the family in supporting and assisting Saudi women working in new non-traditional jobs. The respondents emphasized the importance of the family's role in supporting and assisting Saudi women working in new non-traditional jobs. For example, the respondent No. (7) said: *"Certainly, the family is the first supporter of the working woman, and the family's support takes many forms. It may be moral support, support women, and encourage them to be creative and developed, and support may be material and support women with the material and financial matters that they need to engage in the labor market".* Likewise, the respondent No. (1) said: *"In my opinion, the family plays an effective role in supporting working women, by being the supporter that women depend on when needed, and not abandoning them in bad circumstances, and support her in accomplishing some of the tasks that are difficult for her to accomplish, and cooperating with her in accomplishing some tasks."*

These responses confirm that the family plays an effective role in supporting the working woman, and this may be through material, moral and psychological support for the working woman, cooperating with her in accomplishing some tasks, and constantly encouraging her others. For all the respondents' responses, see the following table:

Table 4

Interviewees' responses to a question about the role of the family in supporting and assistance Saudi women working in new unconventional jobs

Interviewee No.	Response
Interviewee No.1	In my opinion, the family plays an effective role in supporting working women, by being the supporter that women depend on when needed, and not abandoning them in bad circumstances, and support her in accomplishing some of the tasks that are difficult for her to accomplish, and cooperating with her in accomplishing some tasks.

Interviewee No.2	Certainly, the family plays an important role in supporting working Saudi women, by supporting them psychologically and encouraging them to be an active person of society.
Interviewee No.3	Yes, the family plays an active role in empowering working women and their success, by providing them with support and assistance, and easing their household burdens.
Interviewee No.4	Certainly, the family has an important role in the development and superiority of women, and this may be through psychological and moral support, encouragement, and pride in them, and not undermining them and their capabilities.
Interviewee No.5	Yes, the family is an important influence in the life of the working woman, and the impact may be positive or negative on the working woman.
Interviewee No.6	The family certainly has great importance in supporting working Saudi women, starting from their acceptance of women's work and reaching their support in facing the challenges that the job poses to them.
Interviewee No.7	Certainly, the family is the first supporter of the working woman, and the family's support takes many forms. It may be moral support, support women, and encourage them to be creative and developed, and support may be material and support women with the material and financial matters that they need to engage in the labor market.
Interviewee No.8	Certainly, the family is of great importance in empowering women and raising their level.
Interviewee No.9	In most cases, the family greatly influences the support of working Saudi women, and the most important contribution to the family that women need is moral and psychological support, especially in Saudi society.
Interviewee No.10	Yes, the family is the main supporter of working Saudi women, especially in non-traditional jobs, and the role of the family may vary according to the needs of the working woman. For me, the role of my family, as I said, is to represent their care for my children, my husband's interest in me, and his constant accompanying me in the most difficult situations.

- ***Question 5:*** *What are the motives and advantages that you saw in this work?*

To discuss the factors that affect the acceptance of Saudi women in new non-traditional jobs, the researcher asked another question about the motives and advantages that the respondents saw in this work. All respondents had motives and advantages provided by the jobs they chose, but these features and motives differ from one woman to another. Post No. (4) said: *"Certainly, there are many advantages and privileges that I have obtained through my work, the most important of which is the strengthening of the position of Saudi women in society, the refinement of my personality, and the development of my expertise, in addition to the incentives and good financial reward."* While the respondent No. (10) said: *"The most important motivator in this job is the feeling of satisfaction and self-importance through helping and treating patients, in addition to learning everything new in the field of medicine and developing my medical skills and knowledge, in addition to the high income that I get".*

While the respondent No. (5) explained that the main motive for accepting this job is her ability to help her family in covering their obligations, as she said: *"The main motive for accepting this job is to support my family and help them cover the financial obligations. In addition, this job contributed to developing my personality and making me a strong woman."*

For the rest of the respondent's answers, the following table shows the answers of all the women interviewed regarding the motives and advantages that you saw in this work.

Table 5

Interviewees' responses to a question about the factors that affect the acceptance of Saudi

women in new non-traditional jobs

Interviewee No.	Response
Interviewee No.1	First, it is a job in a field of work that I love and I have good knowledge in this field, through which I will gain new experience and knowledge, in addition to enhancing my self-confidence, and enhancing my confidence that I am a Saudi woman who is able to enter the labor market and prove the personality and status of Saudi women.
Interviewee No.2	The main reason for accepting this job is to make my mark in Saudi society and to be a working woman who has her position and importance in society. As for the advantages that this job offered me, they are good financial income, getting to know new people and developing my personality and development.
Interviewee No.3	The main motive for accepting this job is to prove to Saudi society that Saudi women, like any other woman in the world, are able to drive cars efficiently.
Interviewee No.4	Certainly, there are many advantages and privileges that I have obtained through my work, the most important of which is the strengthening of the position of Saudi women in society, the refinement of my personality, and the development of my expertise, in addition to the incentives and good financial reward.
Interviewee No.5	The main motive for accepting this job is to support my family and help them cover the financial obligations. In addition, this job contributed to developing my personality and making me a strong woman.
Interviewee No.6	I told you previously that the main motive for my work in this field is my passion for beauty and cosmetics, as this job enabled me to keep abreast of all developments in the field of beauty and cosmetics, and at times, I get free samples from some companies. In addition to obtaining an employee discount through which I can Buying cosmetics at discounted prices, in addition to having a good financial income.
Interviewee No.7	My first motivation to work in this job is my talent and creativity in this field, in addition to the high financial income that I get from this job.

Interviewee No.8	First, education is the highest profession that a woman can pursue, as she is the one who graduates scientists, doctors, engineers, and others. This job has helped me to expand my knowledge, gain new knowledge and information, and deal with different personalities, along with a good financial income.
Interviewee No.9	I gained many benefits and incentives through my work in this job, the most important of which is the feeling of pride in achieving justice and fairness to the oppressed. In addition to my knowledge of my rights and duties and knowledge of what may expose me to legal favoritism and avoiding it, in addition to the incentives, material rewards, medals and promotions that I have obtained.
Interviewee No.10	The most important motivator in this job is the feeling of satisfaction and self-importance through helping and treating patients, in addition to learning everything new in the field of medicine and developing my medical skills and knowledge, in addition to the high income that I get.

Based on the respondents' responses, we can state that there are many motives that affect the acceptance and rejection of a job, and the most important of these motives are that the job is in a field of work that women love and has good knowledge and experience in the job field, in addition to obtaining a good financial income, and empowering Saudi women in society. the local. In addition, working Saudi women have achieved many advantages through their work in current jobs, the most prominent of which are gaining new experience and knowledge, enhancing self-confidence, developing the status of women in Saudi society, and getting to know new people.

- *Question 6: Do you have any reservations about your work?*

In order to investigate the challenges that Saudi women may face during their work in new non-traditional jobs, the researcher asked another question to the respondents about the extent of reservations about the current job.

The majority of respondents agreed that there are no reservations about the job, and in contrast, the respondent No. (2) said: "*There are some reservations when dealing with male clients, but in general, clients are more acceptable."* While the respondent No. (3) said: *"My reservations about this job are that I was subjected to some harassment from drivers while practicing my profession."* This is consistent with the response of the respondent No. (5), who said: *"Yes, there are some reservations. Sometimes we are harassed by the visitors of the mal"l.* As for the respondent No. (10), she said: *"There are some reservations such as that work does not have specific hours. So I have to be at work whenever they need me."*

For the rest of the respondent's answers, the following table shows the answers of all the women interviewed regarding the reservations about the work.

Table 6

Interviewees' responses to a question about the reservations about work

Interviewee No.	Response
Interviewee No.1	There is no
Interviewee No.2	There are some reservations when dealing with male clients, but in general, clients are more accepting.
Interviewee No.3	My reservations about this job are that I was subjected to some harassment from drivers during the exercise of my profession.
Interviewee No.4	No, I have no reservations.
Interviewee No.5	Yes, there are some reservations. Sometimes we are harassed by the mall visitors.
Interviewee No.6	No, I have no reservations about my job.
Interviewee No.7	No, I have no reservations about my job.
Interviewee No.8	No, I have no reservations about my job.
Interviewee No.9	No, I have no reservations about my job.
Interviewee No.10	There are some reservations like the work has no set hours, so I have to be at work whenever they need me.

- ***Question 7:*** *What are the problems and challenges you faced?*

In this context, the researcher posed another question related to identifying the problems and challenges faced by Saudi women during their work in non-traditional jobs. The majority of the respondents indicated that they faced many challenges during their work. Respondent No. (1) said: "I definitely faced some challenges, especially at the beginning of my career, where it was difficult to deal with my colleagues of the opposite sex, and they also had difficulty at the beginning of dealing with me as a co-worker." While respondent No. (2) said: "*Yes, of course, I faced some challenges when I started this work, most notably the mockery of Saudi women's ability to drive, and the non-acceptance of some Saudi men to lead women.*" Likewise, the respondent No. (10) said: "*Despite the importance of my job and my love for it, I faced many challenges during this work, the most important of which was the difficulty of balancing work and home, staying away from home for long hours, and staying away from my children, not setting specific working hours, and shifts.*" On the other hand, the respondent No. (7) indicated that she was not exposed to any challenges, as she said: "*I did not have any challenges thanks to my family's continuous support.*"

For the rest of the respondent's answers, the following table shows the answers of all the women interviewed regarding the problems and challenges faced by Saudi women during their work in non-traditional jobs.

Table 7

Interviewees' responses to a question about the problems and challenges faced by Saudi women

during their work in non-traditional jobs

Interviewee No.	Response
Interviewee No.1	Certainly, I faced some challenges, especially in the beginning of my career, as my colleagues of the opposite gender were difficult to deal with, and they also faced difficulty in the beginning of dealing with me as a co-worker.
Interviewee No.2	Yes, of course, I faced some challenges when I started this work, most notably the mockery of the ability of Saudi women to drive, and the lack of acceptance of some Saudi males for women driving.
Interviewee No.3	There are many challenges that I encountered during my work, the most important of which are vehicle breakdowns, running out of fuel, the trainee's fear of the extent of my ability to teach her to drive, and society's lack of acceptance of women driving.
Interviewee No.4	As a working woman, I faced many challenges, most notably the difficulty of work and the great responsibility that was entrusted to me, the jealousy of some co-workers, the lack of acceptance by some employees that the CEO was a woman.
Interviewee No.5	The most prominent challenges are the local community's view of the work of Saudi women, harassment by some mall visitors, and male employees.
Interviewee No.6	In fact, there are few challenges in my field of work except for the Saudi society's lack of acceptance of the work of Saudi women.
Interviewee No.7	I had no challenges thanks to my family's constant support.
Interviewee No.8	There are many challenges, the most important of which is the difficulty of balancing work and home, male colleagues not accepting female employees, and male students do not accept that their teacher is female.
Interviewee No.9	Certainly, my field of work is full of challenges, the most important of which are the society's view of this job as a monopoly for men, the difficulty of the tasks that I carry out, the difficulty of balancing between home and work.
Interviewee No.10	Despite the importance of my job and my love for it, I faced many challenges during this work, the most important of which is the difficulty of balancing work and home, being away from home for

	long hours, being away from my children, not setting specific work hours, shifting shifts.

Through the previous responses of the respondents, it is clear that there are many challenges facing Saudi women during their work, the most important of which is the lack of society's acceptance of Saudi women's work, exposure to male harassment in the surrounding community, in addition to the difficulty of balancing work and home. This is consistent with the study of Marican, Borhanuddin, & Abdullah (2009) which showed that the most documented challenge for working women is balancing work and family.

- ***Question 8:*** *How have these problems affected you?*

The researcher also raised a question about the impact of these challenges on working Saudi women. All respondents agreed that these challenges have a significant impact on the personality of women and their ability to address issues and challenges in the best possible way. Respondent No. (1) said: "*I felt frustrated and hopeless in my ability to overcome these challenges, and sometimes I felt that I had to quit this job, but with the passage of time, I was able to overcome these challenges*". She said: "*These challenges had a great impact on my personality, as these challenges made me a stronger woman, able to face difficulties and deal with things in the best way.*"

While both respondents No. (8) and respondents No. (10) agreed that these challenges have contributed to organizing time and being able to balance work and home.

For the rest of the respondents' answers, the following table shows the answers of all the women interviewed regarding how these problems and challenges affect Saudi women while they work in non-traditional jobs.

Table 8

Interviewees' responses to a question about the impact of these challenges on working Saudi women

Interviewee No.	Response
Interviewee No.1	I do not hide you at first I felt frustrated and despairing of my ability to overcome these challenges, and at times I felt that I had to resign from this work, but with time, I was able to overcome these challenges.
Interviewee No.2	These challenges had a huge impact on my personality, as these challenges made me a stronger woman who is able to face difficulties and handle things in the best way.
Interviewee No.3	These challenges affected my personality and ability to connect with others and understand their concerns.
Interviewee No.4	These challenges have affected me in refining my personality and enhancing my ability to assume great responsibilities and address challenges and work issues in the best way, and this was reflected in improving my ability to address family problems and issues in the best way as well.
Interviewee No.5	Certainly, these challenges had a great impact on my personality and enabled me to deal with various personalities and address work issues appropriately.
Interviewee No.6	These challenges made me more daring and strong, I no longer fear what people say and what they will say about me and my work, and I ignore negative people and their words.
Interviewee No.7	I did not face any challenges, but this work contributed to building my personality and enhancing my self-confidence as a productive person and a contributor to the development of society.
Interviewee No.8	These challenges enabled me to balance things and organize my time in the best way, in addition to developing my personality and ability to ignore negative people and sayings.
Interviewee No.9	My work was of great importance in building my character and making me a strong leader, and this job also contributed to developing my ability to accomplish difficult tasks.
Interviewee No.10	At times, these challenges were a source of anxiety and stress for me. However, it was the most important factor in developing my personality and achieving my professional development, and my ability to organize my time despite the shift work system.

- ***Question 9:*** *What are the possible solutions you have thought of?*

The researcher also asked a question regarding the possible solutions that the respondents thought of to address the challenges they faced. Respondent No. (2) said: "I thought of many solutions to meet these challenges, the most important of which was accepting the opinions of others openly and not allowing them to affect my work, in addition to accepting the help of others when I need help." As the respondent No. (3) said: At first, I thought about resigning from the job and this was the easiest solution, but later I thought of facing these challenges by studying how to deal with others and teaching them the basics of leadership easily, studying personal differences between trainees, and dealing with Each trainee according to his personality. In addition to ignoring the abuse and negative people who criticize women's work.

For the rest of the respondents' answers, the following table shows the answers of all the women interviewed regarding the possible solutions you have thought of.

Table 9

Interviewees' responses to a question about the possible solutions that the respondents thought of to address the challenges they faced

Interviewee No.	Response
Interviewee No.1	As I said to you, I thought about giving up the job and submitting my resignation, but this was not the right choice. After that, I decided that I would not be affected by what the others said, nor by the way they dealt, and I would only care about the quality and development of my work, and after that, I began to notice the change of my co-workers and their acceptance of me as an employee like them.
Interviewee No.2	I thought of many solutions to address these challenges, the most important of which was accepting the opinions of others with openness and not letting them affect my work, in addition to accepting the help of others when I need help.
Interviewee No.3	At first, I thought about resigning from the job and this was the easiest solution, but later I thought of facing these challenges by studying how to deal with others and teaching them the basics of

	leadership easily, studying the personal differences between trainees, and dealing with each trainee in a manner appropriate to his personality. In addition to ignoring the abuse and negative people who criticize the work of women.
Interviewee No.4	The most prominent solutions were my diligence and perseverance in work and achieving the best results for the work, in addition to my ignoring the harassment and frustrating statements of colleagues.
Interviewee No.5	The most common way I used to face these challenges was to ignore others, take the seriousness and excel at work.
Interviewee No.6	I was able to meet these challenges by organizing my time, balancing work and home, and ignoring criticism and negative thoughts.
Interviewee No.7	I said that I did not face challenges in my field of work, but I believe that the best way to face challenges is to accept them and be patient in addressing them in the best way.
Interviewee No.8	I faced these challenges by working hard, developing my job skills, and developing my ability to deal with co-workers and male students.
Interviewee No.9	To meet the challenges of work, first, I accepted these challenges, persevered in learning everything new, and proved that Saudi women are capable of taking on important tasks and positions in the country.
Interviewee No.10	I was able to face these challenges thanks to the constant support and support of my family, in addition to my hard work and perseverance, and my attempt to balance my work and family.

- *Question 10: What would have happened if you had not accepted this job?*

In this context, the researcher also raised another question about what would have

happened if the respondents had not accepted this job. Many of the respondents agreed in

answering this question, as most of the respondents answered that if they had not accepted these

jobs, they would be housewives who only take care of household matters. Participant No. (1)

said: "*If I had not accepted this job, I would have stayed at home cleaning the house and

washing dishes, and my personality would not have developed and became his master and I

would have had my mark in Saudi society*", and I agreed on that with the respondent No. (5), who

said: If I had not accepted this job, I would have remained a housewife and would not have been able to help my family cover all the burdens of the house, This is also consistent with the researcher No. (9).

While the respondent No. (2) agreed with the respondent No. (6) in emphasizing that if they had not accepted these jobs, the researcher would not have conducted this interview with them.

For the rest of the respondents' answers, the following table shows the answers of all the women interviewed regarding What would have happened if you had not accepted this job.

Table 10

Interviewees' responses to a question about what would have happened if the respondents had not accepted this job

Interviewee No.	Response
Interviewee No.1	If I had not accepted this job, I would have stayed at home cleaning the house and washing dishes, and my personality would not have developed and became his master and I would have had my mark in Saudi society.
Interviewee No.2	If I had not accepted this job, you would not have done this interview with me.
Interviewee No.3	If I had not accepted this job, I would now be unemployed, and I would not have been able to train many Saudi women to drive.
Interviewee No.4	If I had not accepted this job, I would have remained a regular employee in my previous job, I would not have been able to develop and refine my personality, and I would not have been able to change the view of Saudi society (or a small group of it) towards the work of Saudi women.
Interviewee No.5	If I had not accepted this job, I would have remained a housewife and would not have been able to help my family cover all the burdens of the house.
Interviewee No.6	If I had not accepted this job, I would have been at home and you would not be trying this interview with me, and I would not have been able to keep abreast of developments in the field of beauty and cosmetics.

Interviewee No.7	If I had not worked in this field, I would not have practiced my talents in hairdressing and cutting, and I would not have my own beauty center now.
Interviewee No.8	If I had not accepted this job, I would have remained a teacher in one of the schools, and I would not have been able to develop my knowledge and professional experience.
Interviewee No.9	If I had not accepted this job, I would have become a housewife now without a word or imprint in society, and I would not have become a strong and leading person.
Interviewee No.10	If I had not accepted this job, I would now be a woman who takes care of her home and takes care of her children, who has little role in the development and development of society.

- *Question 11: Did you think about the risks before accepting the job? What are these risks?*

The researcher asked another question that revolves around whether the respondents had previously thought about the risks of working before accepting the job. All respondents confirmed that they thought about the risks of work before accepting the job. Except for the respondent No. (6), who said: "Frankly, I did not think of any risks because of my desire and passion for this field of work."

The most prominent risks that the respondents thought of were the inability to bear workloads, harassment from my co-workers and male clients, the inability to balance work and family, and the possibility of work-related injuries.

For the rest of the respondents' answers, the following table shows the answers of all the women interviewed about whether the respondents had previously considered the risks of working before accepting the job.

Table 11

Interviewees' responses to a question about think about the risks before accepting the job

Interviewee No.	Response
Interviewee No.1	Yes, I thought carefully about what would happen to me if I accepted this job, and I accepted the job and I am satisfied with what will happen to me during my work.
Interviewee No.2	Definitely, an idea in all the risks that I may face while working, the most important of which is my accident while driving, society's lack of acceptance of my work, and my vehicle breaking down in the middle of the road.
Interviewee No.3	Yes, I thought about some of the risks that I might face, such as the vehicle breaking down, my inability to control the trainee, society's lack of acceptance of the nature of my work, and harassment on the road by male drivers.
Interviewee No.4	I certainly thought about the many risks that I might face during my work, the most important of which was my inability to bear the workload, the lack of acceptance by my co-workers.
Interviewee No.5	Yes, I thought about the risks of this job, the most important of which was the local community's view of the nature of my work and the possibility of harassment from co-workers and male visitors.
Interviewee No.6	Frankly, I did not think of any risks because of my desire and passion for this field of work.
Interviewee No.7	Yes, I thought about some risks, the most important of which was customer dissatisfaction with the results.
Interviewee No.8	I certainly thought about some of the risks that I might face, the most important of which is my inability to deal with co-workers, and the difficulty of my ability to bear the workload and balance between my work and my family.
Interviewee No.9	As I told you earlier, my father always reminded me of the dangers of this job, such as my exposure to work injuries, the difficulty of balancing my work and my home, the Saudi society's rejection of the nature of my work.
Interviewee No.10	Of course, I thought about some of the risks that I might be exposed to during my work, which are potential risks for anyone working in my field, the most important of which is my inability to treat the disease, making a medical error during treatment, and being preoccupied with my family and children.

- ***Question 12:*** *In your opinion, do working Saudi women have a role in the cultural and economic development of society? How?*

To achieve the study objective, which revolves around investigating the role of Saudi women working in the cultural and economic development of society. The researcher asked a final question about whether Saudi women have a role in the cultural and economic development of society. All respondents emphasized the importance of women and their role in the cultural and economic development of society. The responses to the posts are included in the following table:

Table 12

Interviewees' responses to a question about the role of Saudi women working in the cultural and economic development of society

Interviewee No.	Response
Interviewee No.1	Certainly, Saudi women have an important role in achieving the cultural and economic development of society, just like the Saudi man, as she accomplishes the tasks assigned to her and achieves profits, development, and sustainability for the institution in which she works.
Interviewee No.2	Of course, Saudi working women have a role in the cultural and economic development of society. This is through her work and her proof that Saudi women, like other women in the world, are able to help men and accomplish difficult tasks.
Interviewee No.3	Yes, of course, the Saudi working woman has a role in the cultural and economic development of society, by making her mark in society and putting forward creative ideas that contribute to the development and development of society.
Interviewee No.4	Yes, Saudi working women have a role in the cultural and economic development of society. When Saudi women assume important positions in the state, they have a prominent role in improving the economy of the institution in which they work. In addition to its role in changing the customs and traditions that restrict Saudi women.
Interviewee No.5	Of course, Saudi working women may have a role in the cultural and economic development of society, perhaps through their role in

	improving the image of Saudi women, raising their status in society and changing the Saudi society's view of working women. In addition, working Saudi women will contribute to the development of the society's economy by promoting female national employment.
Interviewee No.6	The Saudi working woman has an important role in the cultural and economic development of society. This is through her participation in decision-making and her ability to make money on her own, in addition to her role in starting the Saudi society's acceptance of women's work in various fields.
Interviewee No.7	Yes, Saudi working women have a role in the cultural and economic development of society. This is by being a productive woman, who has a source of financial income that enables her to cover her needs without the need to help others.
Interviewee No.8	Of course, Saudi working women have a role in the cultural and economic development of society. This is by doing her job in the best way, and at times beating male co-workers, providing her own source of income.
Interviewee No.9	Yes, Saudi working women certainly have a role in the cultural and economic development of society. That is through her role in improving the image of working Saudi women, and doing their work with the best quality and achieving outstanding work outcomes.
Interviewee No.10	Certainly, Saudi working women have a role in the cultural and economic development of society. This is done by proving that Saudi women are half of society and that they are women capable of working in traditional and non-traditional jobs in Saudi society.

Results

The researcher presented a set of hypotheses that will be validated through the implementation of the current research, the most important of which are the following: Through the data obtained from the participants during the interview, the researcher was able to verify the validity of the hypotheses that she made at the beginning of the study, and these hypotheses revolved around the existence of gender discrimination in new non-traditional work environments and gender bias. Participants confirmed that they suffer from gender discrimination and male bias in their work environments.

This is in line with Gulf News (2017), which states that Saudi women remain excluded from full social participation. In fact, Saudi Arabia remains one of the countries that suffer from gender discrimination. The country has a very high global gender gap rating

With regard to Saudi women obtaining support and assistance from their families, the study assumed that Saudi women do not receive the necessary support and assistance from family and co-workers to achieve a balance between family and work. Nevertheless, through the results of the interviews that were conducted with some of the participants, it became clear that there are many families who provided a lot of support and assistance to Saudi women. This is consistent with Ibrahim (2013), who asserted that Saudi women constitute half of Saudi society, if not more. She is a man's partner in social life. As his mother, sister, daughter, wife, social and financial partner, she is interested in development, growth, and promoting change and prosperity in society. She enjoys the constant support and assistance of the family. While some participants indicated that they did not get support and assistance from their families.

The study also assumed that there is a difference in the factors affecting Saudi working women according to different demographic variables, such as age, marital status, and educational degree. Through the interviews, it was found that although there are many common factors that affect the work of Saudi women, each woman has her own factors and influences that differ from other participants.

The results of the research also confirmed that Saudi women have an important role in the development of society and its economic and social development, and this is consistent with Al-Yousef (2005), who showed that Saudi women are closely linked to the policies of economic growth and human resource development when engaging in the labor market.

Chapter 5: Conclusion and Recommendations

Conclusion

Despite the global interest that women's careers elicit, awareness of women's work is limited in the Arab world. Academic research and studies of many academics seek to identify women's jobs in the United States and European countries, with no interest in women in developing countries in the Arab region. Also in the face of the growing interest in Arab women, most studies focus on specific countries such as Lebanon and the United Arab Emirates, with work in Saudi Arabia clearly limited to women. Given the commonalities among the GCC countries, each country has its own structural realities and distinctive characteristics that require separate studies to gain insight into the specific situations of each country, particularly the experiences of women in each country. This research gap reduces awareness not only of Arab women's experiences but also of the interaction between women's employment and social systems and frameworks. Recently, the Saudi government has also realized the importance of Saudi women. The government paid special attention to raising the status of women in various areas of growth, especially economic growth. The Saudi government's acceptance of the United Nations Charter to help women politically, providing a sound environment for women's work, and opening a women's office in the labor branches of the Ministry of Labor, to improve women's capacity and increase. their participation in economic activities. Targeted high growth rates require the full and efficient use of all economic resources, including human capital. Because women constitute about half of human capital, their active participation in economic activities is of vital importance as this will not only enhance their knowledge and competitiveness but also reduce the country's dependence on foreign labor.

Saudi women play a major role in social and economic transformation within the framework of Vision 2030. The government of the Kingdom of Saudi Arabia is implementing a broad program to reform the status of women that has won international recognition.

A behavioral shift has occurred as many Saudi families have come to realize the importance of women's contribution to the inclusive prosperity of all. In fact, there has been a rapid and tangible improvement over the past few years in the main economic indicators of Saudi women. The participation rates of women in the labor force have increased, and their employment rate has increased significantly.

Saudi women have made huge leaps over the past few years with increased labor force participation rates and private sector employment. Despite these gains, the COVID-19 pandemic has highlighted the challenges that women continue to face in the economy and society today. In addition to social norms and the economic burden of unpaid homework, many women lack work experience and are concentrated in a few sectors and occupations. The government has already implemented several measures to mitigate the impact of the coronavirus crisis, such as providing wage subsidies to Saudis in the private sector. Additional support will be needed during this crisis. This may entail retraining female workers and job seekers on new skills, developing their skills, and providing more remote work opportunities.

Based on the foregoing, working Saudi women suffer from many challenges and obstacles that affect their work in non-traditional jobs, and some of these challenges have been linked to families, such as the family's financial situation. Some wealthy families refuse to work and empower women on the pretext that they do not need money, while there are some Poor family financial conditions that may push women to take jobs that are not suitable for them. In addition, family support greatly affects the work of Saudi women. Some Saudi families do not provide any kind of support and encouragement for women's work, but on the contrary, they work hard to frustrate and marginalize women.

These challenges may also amount to violence that Saudi women may be exposed to, whether verbal or physical violence or any other form of violence that prevents women from working and obtaining a job. Not to mention the masculine distinction that Saudi women suffer greatly. Females in Saudi Arabia suffer from masculine discrimination, where males can work and obtain many powers that women are prohibited from obtaining according to the culture of shame, customs, and traditions, and despite the state's endeavor to achieve women's empowerment., However, shame, traditions, and the phenomenon of defect still exist.

The Kingdom's quest continues to achieve more in an unstoppable ambition within Vision 2030, which aims to raise the rate of Saudi women's participation in the labor market at a high rate, in addition to their holding political positions, as well as their active participation in the Shura Council and the security field, assuming senior positions in the education sector, and nominating themselves for membership in the mayor. Here, we find that empowering Saudi women and supporting their capabilities through rehabilitation and opportunities has made them a real and effective partner in nation building and development. Thus, conducting the current study was of a high degree of importance because it focused on working Saudi women and their role in the development of society and the improvement of its economies. The study presented a scientific addition emphasizing the importance of women in the world and in Islamic and Saudi society, and their role in building society. The study also presented many results and recommendations that stress the need to change Saudi society's view of women and make them partner with men in the development and development of society. The study also emphasized the importance of empowering Saudi women and changing male perceptions of them.

Promoting awareness of the workforce and career issues women face in Saudi Arabia will encourage human resource management departments to enhance Saudi women's work experience by implementing more gender-friendly work environments, practices, and processes. . Therefore, the researcher decided to implement this research to shed light on the role of Saudi women working in community development, to identify the most important challenges and issues facing Saudi women working in new unconventional jobs, and to discuss methods that can be followed to reduce these challenges and issues. To achieve this, qualitative research methods (semi-structured interviews) were used. The researcher conducted a number of interviews with a sample of (10) Saudi women working in new non-traditional jobs.

After the researcher collected the data through the interviews that were conducted with the participants, and then unpacked and arranged them on the "Word" program, the researcher analyzed the data based on content analysis and extracted the required results from the participants' responses. By analyzing the content of the participant's responses, the study reached a number of results, most notably the following:

- Saudi society still rejects Saudi women's work and participation in the labor market, due to customs and traditions that require women to stay at home and take care of their children and family instead of being employed.

- The Kingdom of Saudi Arabia seeks to provide suitable job opportunities for Saudi women and to integrate them into the labor market, and this was evident through the Kingdom's Vision 2030, and work to achieve women's empowerment and support.

- The Kingdom of Saudi Arabia and the Kingdom's vision call for achieving women's empowerment and enhancing their position in society through conferences and seminars related to women's empowerment and providing leadership job opportunities in government institutions for Saudi women.

- The family plays an important role in supporting working Saudi women and helping them achieve career and professional excellence, and this is embodied by motivating them to work and helping them complete their domestic tasks and duties towards the family.

- Saudi women working in new, non-traditional jobs suffer from many challenges, these challenges are male discrimination, violence, and some challenges related to the family.

- The Saudi government has allowed Saudi women to practice many new non-traditional jobs, such as driving a car, joining the army, and many other non-traditional jobs.

- Fear of society's view, norms, and traditions is one of the most important challenges facing Saudi women working in new, non-traditional jobs.

- Fear of not being able to balance work and home is one of the challenges facing Saudi women working in new, non-traditional jobs. Sometimes a woman may feel unable to bear all the duties and obligations that she has towards her family and her work at the same time, and here comes the role of the family in supporting and helping the woman by alleviating some of her burdens and household duties.

- Abuse by male co-workers is considered one of the most prominent challenges facing Saudi women employed in new, non-traditional jobs.

- The exposure of Saudi women employed in a new, non-traditional job to harassment and abuse from other individuals is one of the most prominent challenges facing Saudi women employed in new, non-traditional jobs.

- Saudi female employees are able to face the challenges they face with the help and support of the family.

- Although the challenges facing Saudi female employees are a source of concern and frustration for them, they have a positive impact on building and refining the personality of women and enabling them to deal with issues and challenges with high efficiency.

- The challenges facing working Saudi women affect Saudi women's ability to manage time and balance work and home.

Recommendations

In light of the findings of the study, the researcher recommends a number of the following recommendations:

- The need to change the Saudi society's view of working Saudi women.

- The need for the family to support Saudi women employed in new, non-traditional jobs.

- The necessity of making many transformational changes in employment methods and achieving equal employment opportunities between women and men.

- The necessity of adopting the axes of the Kingdom's vision related to the empowerment and development of women.

- Providing job opportunities for Saudi women and integrating them into the local labor market.

- The necessity of providing appropriate training opportunities for Saudi women employed in new, non-traditional jobs.

- The need for the government to meet the needs of Saudi women working in new, non-traditional jobs.

Future works

Based on the above, the researcher presents some of the suggestions that may be taken in preparing future studies:

- Conducting more studies and research related to identifying the challenges of Saudi women working in new, non-traditional jobs.

- Conducting more studies and research related to studying the directions of the Kingdom of Saudi Arabia towards empowering and supporting women.

- Conducting more studies and research to investigate the opinions of Saudi women about the Kingdom's vision and its impact on changing society's view of women.

- Conducting more studies and research on the factors affecting the success of working women.

www.ingramcontent.com/pod-product-compliance
Lightning Source LLC
Chambersburg PA
CBHW071245020426
42333CB00015B/1636